Agnes —
Keep the night
priorities --- st...
call!

John Budgman
4/26/02

Both of you
can speak!

15 Principles of Success for Business and Life

Time Out...
It's Your Call

John Bridgman

ACW Press
Phoenix, Arizona 85013

Verses marked GNB are taken from the *Good News Bible* Today's English Version, © American Bible Society, Second Edition. 1992.
Verses marked nrsv are taken from *The New Oxford Annotated Bible*, New Revised Standard Version © Division of Christian Education fo the National Council of the Churches of Christ in the United States of America 1991. All rights reserved.

Time Out…It's Your Call
Copyright ©2002 John C. Bridgman
All rights reserved

Cover Design by Eric Walljasper Design
Interior design by Pine Hill Graphics

Packaged by ACW Press
5501 N. 7th Ave., #502
Phoenix, Arizona 85013
www.acwpress.com
The views expressed or implied in this work do not necessarily reflect those of ACW Press. Ultimate design, content, and editorial accuracy of this work is the responsibility of the author(s).

Print permission for *A Charge to Keep*:
325 words from A CHARGE TO KEEP by GEORGE W. BUSH
COPYRIGHT © 1999 by GEORGE W. BUSH
Reprinted by permission of HarperCollins Publishers Inc.
WILLIAM MORROW

Library of Congress Cataloging-in-Publication Data
(Provided by Quality Books, Inc.)

Bridgman, John C., 1937-
　　Time out--it's your call : 15 principles of success
　in business and life / John C. Bridgman. -- 1st ed.
　　p. cm.
　　ISBN 1-892525-68-2

　　1. Success. I. Title.

BF637.S8B75 2002　　　　　　　158.1
　　　　　　　　　　　　　　QBI01-201539

All rights reserved. No part of this book may be reproduced, stored in a retrieval system, or transmitted in any form or by any means–electronic, mechanical, photocopying, recording, or otherwise–without prior permission in writing from the copyright holder except as provided by USA copyright law.

Printed in the United States of America.

Contents

About the Author V
What industry leaders are saying about the author and this book VII
Acknowledgements XI
Foreword XIII

Chapter 1
Priorities & Actions for Success 1

Chapter 2
Action Number One - Give Thanks 3

Chapter 3
The First Priority - Love 13

Chapter 4
Action Number Two - Use The Help 27

Chapter 5
Action Number Three - Share In The Right Way 39

Chapter 6
The Second Priority - Family 49

Chapter 7
Action Number Four - Give Thanks for Priorities & Actions 59

Chapter 8
Action Number Five - Don't Boast, Just Let It Happen 67

Chapter 9
The Third Priority - Joy 73

Chapter 10
Action Number Six - Be Grateful 85

Chapter 11
The Forth Priority - Grace 93

Chapter 12
Action Number Seven - Share The Grace 105

Chapter 13
The Fifth Priority - Forgiveness 117

Chapter 14
Action Number Eight - Keep The Right Priorities 131

Chapter 15
Action Number Nine - Live The Right Life All The Time 143

Chapter 16
Action Number Ten - Follow Me 163

Chapter 17
Using Priorities and Actions 171

Book ordering information 175

About the Author

John C. Bridgman from his own experiences and observations is uniquely qualified to write about priorities and actions for success in business and in life. These experiences are a combination of competition in athletics, leadership in school, business and community and understanding of customers and their needs through numerous sales and marketing positions.

John grew up in Des Moines, Iowa, where he attended Roosevelt High School. He was active in athletics, participating in three sports - football where he was a halfback on the state championship team, baseball as a third baseman and catcher, and swimming where he was a state champion diver and an All American in both swimming and diving. He was also president of the student council.

John attended Iowa State University in Ames, Iowa, where he continued to participate in varsity athletics including baseball and swimming. He also participated in his fraternity and campus activities. He received his BS degree in Industrial Engineering.

Following graduation John joined Cutler-Hammer Inc. in Milwaukee, Wisconsin, and progressed in sales and sales management assignments. He began as a sales engineer in Boston and continued as a branch sales manager in York, Pennsylvania, district manager in Allentown, Pennsylvania, district manager in

Detroit, and regional sales manager in the Midwest. He joined Siemens as the marketing manager for the Control Division in Wichita Falls, Texas.

John joined Asea in White Plains, New York, as General Manager of the Control Equipment Division. After two years of commuting to New York, John relocated the division to Wichita Falls. It was there that he built a company with a "can do" attitude and genuine care for the employees and customers. This division grew rapidly and after the merger with Brown Boveri, John became the first president of ABB Control Inc. This company grew from annual sales of three million dollars to over one hundred million dollars in the year 2000. Presently John is Group Vice President for the Americas for ABB Low Voltage Products and Systems.

John's greatest strength has been his ability to attract talented and high quality people, provide an environment where these talents are appreciated, and focus on taking care of the customer.

Community activities include being an elder and chairman of the board for First Christian Church where he was also named man of the year in 1993. John was president of the Wichita Falls Country Club, president of the University Club, director of the Wichita General Hospital, United Way, Board of Commerce and Industry, Wichita Falls Museum and Art Center, Partners in Education, Wells Fargo Bank and was recently appointed to the board of regents for Midwestern State University by Governor George W. Bush.

John is married to his high school sweetheart Gretchen, and lives in Wichita Falls, Texas. They have three children and six grandchildren living in Kingwood, Texas, San Antonio, Texas, and Glen Ellyn, Illinois.

Here's what industry leaders and others are saying about the author and *Time Out...It's Your Call*

Gordon Rainey, Chairman Hunton & Williams, Richmond, Virginia

> John Bridgman is a highly respected business leader and a deeply religious man. Irrespective of one's religious convictions, the conscientious reader cannot fail to grasp the value of John's sound advice about the role that ethics and consideration of others play in a successful business and personal life.

Dr. John Muir, Retired Minister of The First Christian Church, Wichita Falls, Texas

> When I was privileged to read an early draft of John Bridgman's *Time Out...It's Your Call*, I found myself quoting from the book in a class I was teaching, even before the book was published. The book contains essential keys to successful living.

James Hoggard, Professor of English, Perkins-Prothro Distinguished Professor, Texas Poet Laureate for 2000, Midwestern State University, Wichita Falls, Texas

> In an effort to overcome the fragmentation that's so often a major part of personal life and business dealings, John Bridgman combines motivational and devotional approaches to thought in *Time Out...It's Your Call*. The result is a deeply felt, instructive work.

Jim Coghlin, President of Coghlin Companies, Worcester, Massachusetts

> John, many thanks for providing me with the privilege to review *Time Out...It's Your Call*. Quite frankly, I LOVED IT!
>
> The World is blessed that you have taken the time to put your thoughts to paper, and I am very confident that those who are most fortunate to read *Time Out...It's Your Call* will significantly benefit.
>
> I have already given copies of your stop smoking letter to four of my smoking friends. I think it will help.

Jim Truba, Partner MC2, Detroit, Michigan

> Under your leadership (better stated partnership) I experienced my most productive times. The greatest compliment that I could give you I have already tendered by copying your management style. I would describe it briefly as hire good people, give them direction, recourse them, fight off that which may tie their hands and get out of the way. OK, you might like to follow their activities up on Fridays with a few

wines but that's just showing that you care. I appreciated the opportunity that I have had working with you and look upon it as the apex of my career.

Don Oden, Retired. Retired College Educator and Corporate Executive. Grand Lake, Colorado.

> After reading *Time Out...It's Your Call*, I hope you do understand the reasons I recommended Bob Buford's book *Half Time*:
> #1. You both are successful businessmen, athletes and Christians.
> #2. Both call Texas home.
> #3. Both have been led to focus upon being increasing authentic on the job and off... and especially as we mature.
> #4. You both chose to incorporate Scripture into your personal writings and expand upon it to make your points.

James L. Lundy, Ph.D. President of Performance Systems Inc. and author of acclaimed business books *Effective Industrial Management, Lead, Follow, or Get Out of the Way* and *TEAMS*.

> Wow! What a pleasure it's been to have an opportunity to review your life-enhancing manuscript! The principles and activities you have focused on are so fundamentally sound and universally applicable I believe they could benefit any and every person blessed with the opportunity to study them. They already have been invaluable to me, and I am eager to share numerous copies of your book when it is published. Thanks a bunch! And thanks in advance for making it possible for future readers to enhance their lives, also!

By the way, I took the liberty of giving two smokers copies of the "Dear John" letter you wrote to yourself about smoking. One of them quit smoking within days and is well into the second month of a cigarette-free life! I'm hoping the other one will join the first one soon.

John Humphrey, Chairman, The Forum Corporation, Boston, Massachusetts

Time Out...It's Your Call has a compelling ring of authenticity. These are not abstractions, but guides to live. It makes the book very engaging. It is the author's philosophy of life; very personal. "Take time, take charge, here's how, success awaits." It presents a holistic view. "One life; one model." It reminds me of the old Texas Ranger motto, "One riot, one ranger."

Dr. Jesse Rogers, President of Midwestern State University, Wichita Falls, Texas

Your comments regarding dealing with people as well as many of your other philosophies related to family and faith mean much to me. Please get this manuscript published. It is meaningful and important to managers, administrators, and professionals in all walks of life.

Acknowledgements

My deepest appreciation to my friends and family who have helped me with the writing and editing of this book. Chapter four is "Use The Help," and believe me, I sure have used the help in many ways and from many people.

Very good ideas and suggestions have come from Dr. John Muir of Wichita Falls, Texas, Don Oden of Grand Lake, Colorado, Jim Coghlin of Worcester, Massachusetts, Fruzsina Harsanyi of ABB, Washington D.C., James Hoggard, of Wichita Falls, Texas and Jim Lundy of La Jolla, California and Wichita Falls, Texas.

I thank Dr. Joyce Hinds of Wichita Falls, Texas, and Barbara Arnold of Hilton Head, South Carolina, for sharing their editing and other grammatical talents. Thanks also to Steve Chase of Wichita Falls, Texas for his special talent and expertise in preparing the book for printing.

Special thanks to my family who did proof reading, provided good comments, and were always there with support and encouragement. Thanks to Stephen and Julie Roper of Kingwood, Texas, Jim and Ann Bridgman of Glen Ellyn, Illinois, Chuck and Kristy Bridgman of San Antonio, Texas, my sister Jan Godby of Earlham, Iowa, and my dear mother, Neva Bridgman Wise of West Des Moines, Iowa.

Most of all I want to thank my wonderful wife and best friend Gretchen, for all her love, encouragement, good ideas, sound advice and practical understanding of priorities and actions as they relate to real life.

I am so fortunate to have friends like this and a family so full of love, caring and support. God has surely blessed me in so many ways.

I thank God for all His help and for sharing priorities & actions with me.

Foreword

Taking a time out can be one of the most critical coaching calls in all of sports. Each team has only a few of them to be used during the entire game. When to call a time out and what happens during the time out can change the momentum of the game in either a positive or negative way. Coaches call them and so do officials. Players call them but generally only if something is wrong - such as too many players on the field, time running out, or, in a basketball game, to avoid a turn over. Even the TV networks call them for commercial reasons.

Coaches call time outs for a number of reasons, but usually to make some kind of a change. Or it could be to set up a different play. When they call these time outs, you expect something important to be shared with the team or some significant change to take place.

In pro football, teams can even lose a time out by asking for an instant replay. If the call is not reversed the team loses a time out. Having instant replay is controversial in pro football because it slows the game down and could easily change the momentum for either or both teams. Professional coaches know the importance of having the ability to call a time out when it is needed. Even with this knowledge they will still risk giving up one time out to fix a wrong call in the game.

There are also time outs called in business. Usually these are in meetings, quite often with customers or suppliers, where there is a need for a break to discuss what is happening. One side will call for a time out saying there is a need to meet privately to discuss the offer, the problem or the solution. It is a good strategy, the same as in a sporting event. The difference in business is that there are no formal rules regarding time outs. There is nothing written in the rules of doing business as to the number of time outs that can be called or the length of the time out. A strategically called time out in business can make a tremendous difference in the negotiations. There are business coaches who are masters of timing and strategy and know the right time to call for a time out.

What about calling for a time out in life? Is there a need or a good reason for calling for a time out? Understanding the reason for a time out in sports or in business can be accepted and discussed, but what about a time out in life? How is the need for a time out to be determined? Who knows about this? Who has said "I think we need a time out to get our life in order. We need to make some changes!"

In life, like business, there are also no rules about taking a time out. It is up to each individual to make the call. Each person must recognize the need and determine the right timing for making the call. It might be a tough call, but it doesn't have to be made alone. It is possible to take advantage of instant replays in life and business without the risk of any penalties or losing a future time out.

This book is about taking a time out to learn about priorities and actions that can lead to a happier and more successful life in both business and personal life. *Time Out...It's Your Call* is written to encourage the reader to make the call for a time out from every day pressures and routines to establish the right priorities and take the right actions for a successful life. The 15 principles of success consist of 5 priorities and 10 actions. It is also written to encourage the reader to share his or her own experiences for the next book, which will be *Time Out...It's Your Turn.*

Time Out...It's Your Call

Chapter One
Priorities & Actions for Success

This is a book about being successful in business and personal life. What does success mean? How do you determine what being a success is in both business and life? Can you really combine the two? Can you separate the two? So much of our energy and our time is expended on both business and personal life, yet isn't this combination many times in conflict? Does it make sense that we are one person in business and another person at home? Should we be thinking one way and having values that relate to business, and then have a completely different set of priorities and ethics during the "off" hours? We might even have a business voice that is different from our at-home voice.

We may not realize we are living a kind of double life, but let's think about it. Spend a few minutes comparing your "business" and "personal" life. What kind of responsibilities do you feel for the employees and their families? Are they similar to the responsibilities you feel for your family, friends and neighbors away from work? These questions are meant to start the process of thinking about yourself and your relationships in both business and life. Do you sense any inconsistencies here?

How do you define success? Maybe success is not a final destination or number of achievements obtained, but a journey with different goals reached along the way. I'll argue that what happens at each milestone is what determines success. Success is time-related. Is success defined as happiness, money, a happy, healthy family or a good relationship with God, or what? Is your definition of success different from your neighbor's or your spouse's? Perhaps, but maybe if the real meaning of success were fully known and understood, then there wouldn't be differences. Is it important to learn and accept what success really is during the course of our lives? Yes, of course it is! This knowledge helps determine which actions are necessary to achieve success in both business and life.

What is success? We will not answer this question right now, but helping you define success will be an important part of this book. I hope you will be thinking about what success means to you as you read *Time Out...It's Your Call*. Another point to consider at the beginning stages of our discussions about actions is whether we understand and appreciate priorities. So consider these two subjects - taking specific actions to be successful and establishing priorities. Would these priorities be consistent between your business and personal life? Should they be different? What do you think? The 15 principles of success are these priorities and actions.

We have decided to share this information with you by presenting a list of actions that will lead to the answers you are seeking or may wish to seek. We will also share a list of priorities as we go along. There is an order to this discussion, so please follow along and don't jump ahead or read the last of the book first. This book is for you to use and to share with others. Should you want to be more successful in your business and personal life and want others around you to also be more successful we hope this book will help you. Please keep your family, friends and business associates in your thoughts and prayers when considering these priorities and actions.

Keep an open mind! That way, good thoughts, ideas and expressions of gratitude can easily be received and given. Imagine how much those with closed minds are missing.

Chapter Two
Action Number One

This book is for you, but it is also for those who are struggling and whose lives are confused and painful. It is for all of us. Whatever our particular situation is at this particular time, the first action is to "Give Thanks."

You are probably thinking, give thanks to whom and for what? Where is the most natural place to start? Think about all those who have had positive influences on your life. Have you thanked them for what they have done? Why not thank them now? Maybe you should thank your wife or husband, your mother or father, or even someone at work. Do it today. You might even feel the benefits of the action immediately. Do it openly and honestly with no selfish motives. Expect nothing in return. If you don't feel right about a particular person and your heart is not in it, find someone else to thank. This simple act is just a beginning.

Are there those who aren't with you now whom you regret not saying thanks to in the past? It's not too late to express gratitude. If you are sincere, they will hear and they will know. They probably do already because you have thought about your indebtedness. But say thanks anyway. You surely won't regret it.

Al Comito was my baseball coach in high school. He coached high school and summer baseball which involved many hours of practice, traveling and games. Many of the players became very close to him. He was more than a coach, he became a close friend. I mention this friendship because we all admired him and grew from his influence. During the awards ceremony my senior year in high school, when varsity letters were presented to the athletes, Al Comito took the time to say some nice things about me. The words were thoughtful and touched me deeply. I'm sure my parents felt the same way. But I never said, "Thank you, Coach." I should have expressed my gratitude and I regret not doing so before he passed away. I have said "thank you" now and I'm convinced that Al knows how I feel. You will be assured too if you express gratitude that is overdue. Why not give it a try?

Now think, whom should I give thanks to in my business life? I want to take this action in the right professional way but also in a humble way. It might be best to start small with someone you are comfortable talking to because thanking him or her would be natural. Start making a list of those you have thanked with the reason why and a list of those persons whom you would like to thank over time. Now don't make a list of who thanked you because that is not the purpose for giving thanks. Examples of recommended lists will be shown at the end of each chapter. I want to strongly encourage you to use each list. You don't have to put a lot of time into this or to include a large list of names, but at least do a few. See how it goes. It won't hurt!

I would also suggest making a list of customers or suppliers that you would like to thank for supporting your company, agency or organization. Call them and let them know you appreciate their business and loyalty. Ask how you can do a better job of servicing their account. You should make at least one call like this per week. If you are not in a position to make these calls, why not give this suggestion to your company? Someone should be making these calls.

Try also giving thanks, again in the right way, to people who provide you with some service. Think about how you can thank them so they will know that the sentiment is sincere and not just words. One time I thanked a check-out person and told her she must be having a great day because she seemed to glow. I told her that her happiness helps others to have a better day, as it did me. Happiness is contagious. I could tell she appreciated my comments and I felt better afterwards for simply expressing my thoughts. This act may have taken less than a minute and who knows how many people may have gained from this short conversation — at least two that I know of, and that alone makes it worth-while.

If you can provide these little acts of kindness and say thanks to strangers, shouldn't you be kind and grateful to your spouse every day? How about doing the same for the rest of your family and your business associates?

I learned about a wonderful concept concerning "emotional bank accounts" from our son Jim. He attended a seminar at his church called "Success That Matters." A part of the seminar focused on "finding a new best friend in your wife/husband." As a husband or a wife you have the ability to either make withdrawals or deposits into your spouse's "emotional bank account."

These are examples of deposits:

- Spend quality time together - just the two of you
- Listen to each other deeply
- Touch each other often

- Accept him/her unconditionally
- Be committed to him/her
- Encourage each other
- Take care of each other financially
- Laugh with each other
- Be his/her best friend

With all these deposits the big idea is that after God, but before all others, make him/her the most important part of your life.

These are good examples of deposits. You probably can add to this list. Concentrate on the deposits and eliminate the withdrawals! Give thanks for these opportunities and these deposits that take place every day. I give thanks for the many deposits my wife Gretchen makes to my emotional account!

I've always wanted to do something that was totally unexpected for our employees. When we reached a new milestone in sales we decided to give each employee a one hundred-dollar bill. We grossed up their pay so they actually got the full $100. During an employee meeting we handed out envelopes to each employee and said thanks to each of them for their extra efforts and contributions in helping the company reach this new sales level. The first employee who opened the envelope and pulled out a new one hundred-dollar bill was really surprised. He was shocked and after a moment of silence, he said, "That is what I'd say is really knowing how to say thank you." We have continued this tradition each time we reach a new million-dollar level for sales in a month. The employees will tell you the year 2000 has been a great year. Our employees have shared in our success as we have given each employee $600 for reaching new goals. That's six times in one year. This has been an exciting way to give thanks to our team. All employees received the same reward no matter what their position was with the company.

Now here comes a major concern. Take the time to provide thanks to God for all he has given to you and your family. Go ahead and do it. Do it through prayer. Do it in your thoughts, do it verbally and even do it in writing. He will hear you in all these ways and you'll be surprised at the power behind writing down your prayers. Keep what you have written. But do this by yourself and for yourself. You don't need to share it with anyone or to do it for any other reason than to say to God, "Thanks for all the blessings that You have given to me."

Being grateful and giving thanks can be done over time and should continue and increase because you will continually have more to be grateful for and want to let God know your blessings are increasing.

The first action is to give thanks. Make your own lists with all the information you want to include. Use the ones at the end of the chapter or make up your own. One list will be for those you have thanked, the next for ones you plan to thank, including customers. And always be sure to list the personal blessings God has given to you.

Priorities & Actions
Family, Friends & Associates That I have Thanked

Date	Person Thanked	Reason for Thanking	Reaction or Result

Priorities & Actions
Plans for Giving Thanks

Date	Person to be Thanked	Reason for Thanking	Reaction or Result

Time Out ... It's Your Call

Priorities & Actions
Customers to Thank

Customer Name	Location	Individual	Telephone #	Date	Reaction or Result	Further Action

The First Action

Priorities & Actions
Personal Lists of Thanks

Thanks for These Blessings

Date

Plan to have a good and productive day. Giving thanks will help to make this happen both for you and the recipient of your gratitude.

Chapter Three
The First Priority

What would you say the first priority should be? Most people would say God or family or church or success in life, or even country or health. Some of these could be considered priorities and some blessings, such as good health. Although we can do much to be healthy, with exercise and good eating habit, good health is still a blessing, not a priority.

What do you think is the number one priority in your life today? Try to answer this question in a way that reflects what your top priority is, not what you think it should be. Where are you spending your time and energies? What do you think about most each day?

Are you satisfied with your answer?

There are five priorities that we will discuss in this book, but the first and most important of these is love!

Why is love the most important? I think it is because when Jesus was asked what is the greatest commandment in the Law, he answered:

> Love the Lord your God with all your heart, with all your soul, and with all your mind.' This is the greatest and most important commandment. The second

> most important commandment is like it: 'Love your neighbor as you love yourself.' The whole Law of Moses and the teachings of the prophets depend on these two commandments.
> Matthew 22:37-40

Set your hearts on the most important gifts, but always remember:

> I may be able to speak the languages of human beings and even of angels, but if I have no love, my speech is no more than a noisy gong or a clanging bell. I may have the gift of inspired preaching; I may have all knowledge and understand all secrets; I may have all the faith needed to move mountains — but if I have no love, I am nothing. I may give away everything I have, and even give up my body to be burned — but if I have no love, this does me no good.
>
> Love is patient and kind; it is not jealous or conceited or proud; love is not ill-mannered or selfish or irritable; love does not keep a record of wrongs; love is not happy with evil, but is happy with the truth. Love never gives up; and its faith, hope and patience never fail.
>
> Love is eternal. There are inspired messages, but they are temporary; there are gifts of speaking in strange tongues, but they will cease; there is knowledge but it will pass. For our gifts of knowledge and inspired messages are only partial; but what is perfect comes, then what is partial will disappear.

When I was a child, my speech, feelings and thinking were all those of a child; now that I am an adult, I have no more use for childish ways. What we see now is like a dim image in a mirror; then we shall see face to face. What I know now is only partial; then it will be complete — as complete as God's knowledge of me.

Meanwhile these three remain; faith, hope, and love; and the greatest of these is love. 1 Corinthians 13:1-13

It is then love that you should strive for. Set your hearts on spiritual gifts, especially the gift of proclaiming God's message. 1 Corinthians 14:1

The first priority is love, followed by family; but the two should go together.

Should the priorities in business and personal life be the same? "Love your neighbor" means a lot. Certainly all those people you work with each day should be considered at least as important to you as neighbors. This is the answer to the question.

If you could look ahead to the time right before you die and reflect back on your life, what do you think you would be thinking? Would you be saying that you should have spent more time working, or had a different job, or should have made more money? I don't think so. These last thoughts will be about the important priorities that should have been in your life. These thoughts would be about love. Love for God and his love for you, and love for family, friends and associates will be what I think those thoughts will be about: "I should have spent more time sharing my love with those that I love." Or "I am so thankful that I had the love of those I also loved." Do you think these would be your thoughts or would they be different? What would you like people to say at your eulogy? What would you like people to say at your 50th wedding anniversary?

I would think we would also want to look back at our business careers and reflect on what has been accomplished. I really do think at this time it will again be most important to enjoy and remember the good relationships and good times spent with fellow workers and customers. These reflections probably won't be ones of progressing from an engineer to senior engineer to engineering supervisor to manager of engineering or even the number of patents held, but will be reflections on the relationships with people and friendships with team members over the years. We will remember people - not things.

In business the priorities are the same. The first priority is love for your fellow employees, for those that you manage and for those who manage you. This kind of love is different from your love for your spouse or your children, but it is still love. It should also include love for the job. You don't have to love the job one hundred percent of the time, but you better love a good part of it if you are going to be a loving, caring person at business and at home. There's no doubt about it — loving, caring organizations attract and keep the best employees and get the best results.

What is love in business and how do you show and express your love? Let's look back at I Corinthians for some help with this.

"Love is patient and kind." It is important in business each day to take the time to listen to associates and customers, to listen to not only what they are saying, but also why they are saying it. All of us are busy, with much on our minds, so it takes commitment to be patient and kind when people come into the office to talk about their needs, their problems or their projects. It's hard to just turn off what we're doing and give full attention to a fellow worker. The same goes for a phone call or an e-mail. Be patient and kind with all of these three means of communications - face to face, on the phone, or on e-mail. A good way to practice being "patient and kind" is to follow this advice about being a thoughtful and considerate listener.

If you have a problem to discuss or a complaint about what has happened, handle it face to face. Speak only when you know you are ready to communicate in the right way. Take your time; don't be too quick to complain. Good news can be shared personally, in oral or in written form, but bad news should be given only personally in the right setting, and if face-to-face is not possible then verbally, but never just in writing. In a similar way, consider who else should receive copies of this information. Here especially it is important to be kind and respect the feelings of others. You want to be supportive and encouraging to the ones you love. In these days of e-mail, where it is so easy to send copies to others, be thoughtful about who receives your correspondence. Make sure your e-mail is clear and can be easily understood by all those receiving it.

Never be unkind or show lack of respect to a fellow employee so that he or she loses face within the company or with other business associates. There is no order or project that would be worth this!

Knowledge is: Talking less and being a good listener.

Love is: Listening to what is really being said and meant, not just listening to the words.

"Love is not jealous or conceited or proud." Isn't this a good description of someone whom you like to be around at work? Someone who wants you to get the credit for what you have done and someone who is humble. Really no one enjoys being with someone who is conceited. So here again it is a two-way situation, where you will not want to be jealous or conceited or proud, but likewise you will want to love those fellow workers who will learn right ways from your example. Help them learn that they don't need to be jealous, conceited or proud to be successful.

"Love is not ill-mannered or selfish or irritable". Be of good spirits at work. Have a good time. Have a sense of humor. Don't take yourself too seriously. If you happen to be in an irritable mood, do something about it; just don't waste a precious day in a bad mood. Have you noticed that when you are in a good mood, others often are too? Isn't this the way with your children also? Could it be that good moods are contagious? If you have an associate who is having "one of those days," do something about the problem. It might be the time to do something special and unexpected for this person. Does he or she like hot fudge sundaes or funny cards? Why not have one of these delivered to his or her desk with a note saying, "Because I care" or "Smile, you're on Candid Camera" or something light that would be appropriate. Sign it or not, it's up to you. It will mean more if you sign it and then you avoid the risk of the gesture being viewed as being sarcastic.

"Love does not keep a record of wrongs." How appropriate is this idea for business life? It is okay to make mistakes. In fact, it is healthy and necessary because how else would you and others learn? If you always waited to make sure you would not make a mistake, nothing would get done. When mistakes happen, don't make someone live with his or her "wrongs." Don't punish yourself either by dwelling on mistakes you have made. Forget them and move on, making sure you have learned from what happened. Forgive someone if that is the right thing to do, if the mistake personally affected you. Love remembers and appreciates the past, but grows and thrives on the present and the future. Why? Because we can show our love in the present and in the future. It is something that we can influence.

There is another truth here which this translation misses and this is important in our relationships, both in business and in daily life. The New English Bible translates this passage from 1 Corinthians 13:6, "Love keeps no score of wrongs; does not gloat over other men's sins, but delights in the truth." In short, this means that one does not take satisfaction when a fellow worker messes up, making one's self look better by comparison. Instead the employee should honestly rejoice when another person does well, without resentment. To respond in this way is to be secure in life itself.

My mother proposed a toast at a surprise birthday party we gave for our friends a few years ago. Although it's been widely used, I would like to share it again because it seems to fit. "Yesterday is a memory, tomorrow is a promise, today is a gift and that is why it is called the present."

Love never gives up. I think we are too quick to give up on someone in business. If results are not what is expected or wanted, it is easy to look for someone to blame or someone to replace. Sometimes this has to be done, but often if we would only take the time to be patient and know the individual, things could be done differently. You know no one is perfect or ideal for the job. Everyone has strengths and weaknesses, no matter what the position. The loving organization recognizes this and knows that each individual is say ... 85% positive for the job and 15% not so positive. Good organizations stress the 85% abilities and minimize the 15% areas by giving support or getting someone else to do the 15% tasks. Remember the song: "Accentuate the positive - eliminate the negative....It's a catchy song with a catchy message!

This strategy makes sense, doesn't it? With the difficulty in finding real talent now, why not keep the 85% talent rather than lose this for the 15% problem area? Concentrate on using the strengths and avoid using the weaknesses as much as possible. At least recognize them and accept the consequences as your responsibility also.

You have probably heard about the snake that asked the Indian to carry him down the mountain and told him he wouldn't bite him. When they arrived at the base of the mountain, the snake bit him and the Indian said, "I thought you said you weren't going to bite me." The snake replied, "You knew I was a snake when you picked me up so you should have expected me to behave like a snake." Take into consideration the strengths and weaknesses of your business associates and take actions to compensate for their weaknesses. And don't hire snakes! You know some companies do.

These are some of the ways love shows up in the business world. Very much like love in our personal life, isn't it? Remember: "Love is patient and kind; it is not jealous or conceited or proud; love is not ill-mannered or selfish or irritable; love does not keep a record of wrongs" 1 Corinthians 13: 4-7.

Right now take a few minutes thinking about those whom you spend most of your time with in business each day. How many of them do you love, like, not like or just not have any feelings about at all? Let's work on this mental list or use the form at the end of the chapter as a guide. Are there enough on the "love" list? How large a list is this? Think about all those on the "like" list and think about what you could do to move them to the "love" list. How would you treat them differently? Then move to the "indifferent" list and see how you could move them to the "like" list. This change shouldn't be too hard, should it? It probably can be accomplished by just taking the time to get to know the individuals better. What did Will Rogers say? "I never met a man I didn't like." Look at who Jesus took as his disciples! They probably wouldn't have made your "love" or "like" lists in the beginning.

Then take those who are on the "don't like" list. Why are they on this list? Is it something they do or have done, or is it something you have done? Maybe there needs to be forgiveness on your part or a new humility to start the movement from "don't like" to "like" and then later on to "love."

Sometimes we get upset with something that has happened or with what someone said, and a negative attitude continues because no one makes the first move to change it. It could be pride or anger or maybe even a misunderstanding that is standing in the way of being on each other's "like" or "love" list.

Just a few weeks ago we were entertaining some visitors for lunch at the Branding Iron, a local Wichita Falls barbecue restaurant. You would enjoy it, but don't take your American Express Card or Visa or MasterCard, because they only take cash. We were discussing the kinds of restaurants that are most popular and someone mentioned that in Wichita Falls people go to dinner early and usually only drink iced tea. I jokingly said that it is because of the high population of Baptists. With this comment, a good friend of mine for over 20 years responded that Baptists could drink if they wanted to. I felt like I had offended this friend by my inappropriate comment. Rather than worry about this, I went to see him that same afternoon and apologized for what I had said. "I didn't mean to be critical," I said. "In fact drinking iced tea for dinner is a good thing, not a bad thing." He laughed and said, "You didn't upset me at all."

The message here is that maybe this could have been a small thing that upset him or I could have worried about it for a long time. So don't take the chance of having an offense happen. Do something about it as soon as possible. If there is any question about upsetting someone by something you said or did, take corrective action. I know I sure felt better after talking to my friend about this and I think he appreciated my interest in him and his feelings.

When I was growing up in Des Moines, I had a neighbor, Jim Fleming, who was my buddy and we did a lot together. One day we got into an argument and we didn't speak to each other for probably six months. One day our family had an extra ticket to a Drake University basketball game and my parents suggested I ask Jim to join us. I called him and he accepted. That night we couldn't even remember why we were mad at each other. Do you have situations like that or do you know those who do and maybe they need to be invited to a basketball game? What should you do about the situation or what should you do to help?

My dad used to say, "Never let your anger or pride cost you money or a friendship." I would also add, "Don't let it put a flaw in your character." Even better is to ask what would Jesus do in this situation? Isn't this approach great? Take time to consider this question when a difficult and trying situation presents itself: Don't do something that moves you from their "love" or "like" list to their "don't like" list.

Now for some personal analysis. Which lists do you think you are on? If you have many on your "like" lists, you will probably be on many "like" lists, and if you have many on your "don't like" lists, you probably are on as many "don't like" lists. In reality, the "love" lists are usually pretty small and the "indifferent" lists are the largest. Let's get started with moving up the lists and see if you don't find the same thing happening to you and the lists you are on. Obviously others won't be having these mental lists, but they will be having real-life, real-time, real-action lists that you and others can see. By their actions and your actions you will know where you stand and when you have moved from one list to another. Remember, the goal is to move up, not down - for you and for your associates.

Thinking about these lists reminds me of the story about a young couple considering moving to a new city. They stop to ask a senior citizen, "Is this a friendly city and are the people friendly here?" His answer was a question to them: "Are they friendly in your city?" They answered, "Yes, they are." and his reply was, "They are also friendly here." This story relates to "your" lists and "their" lists. Like most avenues in life, the lists are also two-way.

Some advice here. Don't just pick out the easy people to put on your "love" and "like" lists; pick out some who are difficult and maybe not so attractive. Show them the love you have for them at work. I think the satisfaction and results from these will be far greater than the most popular, most attractive fellow workers. It's easy to love a lovable person, but what does that gain you or them? Whom did Jesus pick? Who really needs our love and our support at work? Whom would Jesus pick for his list at your place of business? Whom would He sit with at lunch?

You know you really don't have to wait until late in life to look back and reflect on your priorities. You can reflect now when you still have the time and ability to change your priorities or to strengthen them. Consider now the number one priority, which is love. Is love your number one priority in your business and in your life?

All of us are different and it is clear that we are also at different stages of individual growth, development, education, experience and understanding. These priorities and actions are for all levels of personal and business life. Some will be more timely and important to you depending on where you are and what your needs are today. The priorities are still priorities and they are in the right order. The actions are not necessarily in an order of importance and this will vary from person to person.

Priorities & Actions
Love List

	Indifferent	Don't Like	Like List	Love List
Friends and Associates				
Business				
Life				

Be ready and prepared to receive good news, powerful directions and God-given gifts. Make good use of all these blessings

Chapter Four – Action Number Two
Use the Help

The first action is to Give Thanks and the first priority is Love. After reading these two chapters and working on some of your own lists, how do you feel about where we are going? Did you notice we used "we" again? You might not have been aware of this pronoun earlier, so let me repeat key sentences so you don't have to thumb back to the beginning of the book.

We will not answer this question right now, but defining success for you will be an important part of this book.

We have decided to share this information with you by presenting a list of actions that will lead to the answers you are seeking or should be seeking. We will also share a list of priorities as we go along.

The reason for "we" is that I really don't believe that one does something alone or accomplishes anything worthwhile alone. You always have help. This chapter is about using that help in business and in life.

The "I" word has always bugged me. Listening to someone say "I can ship this for you today" just isn't right. The right answer is "we" can ship this for you today. In business as in life there isn't the "I" possibility of accomplishing anything totally alone.

You always need, and generally get, some level of help from someone or Someone.

After Asea, a Swedish electrical manufacturer, relocated its operation from Yonkers, New York, to Wichita Falls, Texas, and Stromberg was acquired and also relocated to Wichita Falls from Cleveland, we had a problem with some of the managers using the "I" word too much. To make them aware of this, we started an "I kitty" where anyone during a staff meeting who used the "I" word had to put a quarter in the kitty. You know this exercise worked. It even changed the attitude of a number of managers and led to our becoming a "we" company throughout the entire organization. A sense of teamwork was accomplished with a lot of kidding in an atmosphere of good feelings.

There is only one time when using the "I" word is right and that is when you do something wrong or make a mistake. Then the pronoun should be I, even if the cause of the problem wasn't just you, and it probably wasn't. It is okay to accept the responsibility and the blame.

Help can come from anywhere and many times from where you least expect it. Think about what happened to us once when we were trying to create a slogan for our mission and vision statement for our company. The creative people came up with "Customer First, Quality First." This was good, but still lacked the punch we really wanted. When we reviewed this in our staff meeting, our CFO, Bill Merkel, said, "Why don't we make it 'Customer First...Quality Always.' " This slogan was right and everyone in the meeting knew it immediately. Here was the answer we were looking for and it came from an accountant. Thanks, Bill!

Every organization, every company and every family has a wealth of talent ready to be used. Why don't we use it? Why don't we use the help that is there anxiously ready and willing, if only people are asked in the right way. **Use the help!** You will be amazed with the results you will receive because good ideas can and will come from all over and from many different people. You know it doesn't matter where the good ideas or the help comes from; what is important is that it comes. Don't forget to give thanks for the help because you want it to continue.

You don't need to struggle with a problem alone; it is okay to ask for help. Let others share in the problem-solving process. Let them know what the real problem is and see what ideas they might have. There isn't a need for a lot more meetings to involve them; sharing can be done in a quiet way and even with just a few minutes of discussion. I have found over the years that if you have a problem or situation that isn't right, if you put as many facts as possible in front of you and then don't think about it for a while, your subconscious mind will work on the problem and answers will come. Likewise, others can do the same for you if you involve them. Let many subconscious minds work on the problem.

Where else do you need to use the help? Think about what you do well and what you do very well. Take a minute and write these things down. Write them down for business and for life. Are they different? Think about what you don't do so well and also write them down. You should now have two lists and hopefully the first is longer than the second. Possibly you can use your latest performance review for those business-related strengths and weaknesses.

I would ask you to make two more lists. The first is, what do you most like doing at work and in life? The second is, what do you least like doing? Compare these lists and what do you see? Is there any similarity between the list of your strengths and what you most like doing? There probably is and there probably should be. I would think it is the same for the things you don't like to do and what you think you don't do so well.

Perhaps you are thinking, why did I do that and what does that have to do with using the help? The answer is to use the help that is available for those areas where you need it. An example might be that you feel you are very good at leading and motivating people, but you are not good at giving performance reviews. Did I hit a hot button? Is this pretty close to home? It is for me. But you know not wanting to give performance reviews doesn't make sense. How can a person be good at leading and motivating and not good at talking to people about their performance? What you are probably not good at is preparing for the performance review, not giving it. You must enjoy talking with your people about themselves, their careers, their opportunities and areas where they need improvement. Use the help in preparing the performance review. Use your human resource manager if you have one to help you prepare the review - she or he is probably very good at that, so why not use this strength and this talent? It will be a win - win situation for both of you and, most importantly, for the employee being reviewed.

You can use this example for almost all situations. You still have the responsibility for the functions and tasks, but you can use the help available within your organization to strengthen and supplement your abilities and interests.

Now go back to your lists. Next to the items on the list of what you don't like to do write down where you will "use the help" and what way you will use it so that the item can move to the "like to do" list.

You have done this and now I am going to ask you to do something else with these lists that will probably surprise you and maybe even excite you after you have done it. Take the lists which you made that show the things that you are very good at and what you most like to do. Think about how you can share these with others in your company, your organization or your family. How can others "use the help" from you? This isn't easy because you just don't run up to a business associate and say, "I am really good at giving motivational talks and you aren't, so I am going to help you." No, there is a lot more to it than that. We hope this book will help give the answers to how business associates can help each other.

I think we can all help each other by communicating openly and clearly. There is a real art to good communicating, but everyday business communications should be easy. My feelings on communications are pretty simple. If I can't completely understand what is being said or asked then I'm pretty sure that there is a fairly high percent of those receiving the communications who won't either. The communication has to be clear and easily understood. Everyone receiving the communication should know what he or she is supposed to do with it. Who has the ball?

ABB (Asea Brown Boveri), a global technology company, started a program called the reverse mentor program where the top 400 managers in the company are required to select a young employee to have them mentor the manager. They are supposed to mentor the senior managers on computer knowledge, use of Internet, eCommerce and other areas of technology. These senior managers are generally classified as "BC" rather than "AC," which means they grew up Before Computers not After Computers. This reverse mentoring is being done because many of these senior managers need to "use the help" available within our company, but it also is being done so these managers can really get to understand how the younger generation is thinking, what they need, what they desire, and excites them. This is done for two reasons. The first is so that we can learn from them. That will help us attract and retain talented young employees, and the second is so that we can communicate with our present and future customers. This is in no way age discrimination or preferential treatment. It is real life, and in business as in life we need to understand the dynamics of the various generations. We need to help them and they need to help us. It is a wise thing that Goran Lindahl, former CEO of ABB, started. Maybe he also had help with this idea, but it doesn't matter. It is a good idea and ABB and the employees will benefit from it. That is what counts.

You can use the help from many, many people and resources but the most valuable help comes from God. I think so much of "Footprints" by Mary Stevenson.

Footprints

> One night a man had a dream. He dreamed he was walking along the beach with the LORD. Across the sky flashed scenes from his life. For each scene he noticed two sets of footprints in the sand: one belonging to him, and the other to the LORD.
>
> When the last scene of his life flashed before him, he looked back at the footprints in the sand. He noticed that many times along the path of his life there was only one set of footprints. He also noticed that it

happened at the very lowest and saddest times in his life.

This really bothered him and he questioned the LORD about it: "LORD, you said that once I decided to follow you, you'd walk with me all the way. But I have noticed that during the most troublesome times in my life, there is only one set of footprints. I don't understand why when I needed you most you would leave me."

The LORD replied: "My son, my precious child, I love you and I would never leave you. During your times of trial and suffering, when you see only one set of footprints, it was then that I carried you."

Mary Stevenson (1922-1999)

"Footprints" says so much, doesn't it? I cry every time I read it, I think because there is so much truth in it and God wants you to know He is always with you. I also cry every time I see the movie Field of Dreams, and I think this is because I still want to play catch with my dad.

Use the help. Play catch with your children; play catch, so to speak, with your fellow workers and family. Use help and give help. Do it while you can.

Start another list with the names of all those with whom you want to "play catch."

I recently asked Jesus to help me with a business problem. Does that sound presumptuous on my part? Who am I to ask Jesus for help? Well, there was a situation where a decision was made that I didn't feel was right for a number of reasons including the possibility that it would personally affect some people in the wrong way. I was told it would be impossible to have this decision changed. I asked Jesus for help because I didn't think I could do this alone. I know He helped me. Yes, the decision was changed. In business I think it is okay to ask God for help and to use the help if you are asking for help for the right reasons. Why wouldn't God want to help you in business as much as in life? You should use the help from God in business and in life. Don't do it to test God; do it for the right reasons!

We have spent considerable time urging all to "Use the help" there is, but there is another aspect of using help that we should also consider. That is to appreciate the fact that the person who is most inclined to be a "giving" person often has a difficult time receiving. A friend of mine's mother was like that - always helping others but unable to accept help until she was forced to do so by failing health. If we are going to be able to receive God's undeserved gifts of grace, then we should allow others to be givers too, by graciously accepting their gifts.

The first two actions are Give Thanks and Use the Help and the first priority is Love.

Priorities & Actions
Things That I Do Well in Business and/or Life

Things That I Do Well	Business	Life	Who Can I Share With	How Can I Share

Priorities & Actions
Things That I Don't Do So Well in Business and/or Life

Things That I Don't Do So Well	Business	Life	Who Can Help	How Can I Make This Happen								

Priorities & Actions
What I Most Like Doing in Business & Life

Why										
Life										
Business										
Things That I Most Like Doing										

Priorities & Actions
What I Least Like Doing in Business & Life

Why											
Life											
Business											
Things That I Least Like Doing											

Stop, look and listen before crossing a "street" in life. Stop, look and listen to make sure you are on the right path and going in the right direction. The right path is movement to the love list.

Chapter Five – Action Number Three
Share in the Right Way

You have talents, strengths and gifts. You know you do, and in the last chapter you listed at least some of your strengths. You didn't include talents and gifts as a separate list, but now you should be thinking about all of these if we are talking about sharing in the right way. What do we want to share in business and what do we want to share in life? What can we share? We have certain tangible resources that we can share, and we have our own personal resources that we also can share. You know the tangible resources you have and you are probably sharing with your church, United Way, your university or your favorite charity. Or maybe you are planning on doing your share sometime in the future. We are not going to discuss this now. It is a personal thing and up to you to do what you think is right for your own personal situation. It is right, though to think about sharing.

We are going to discuss sharing your talents, strengths and gifts in the right way, which also means for the right reasons.

Let's start by agreeing that in business and in life we really do want to share. Basically all of us are sharing and caring people, and you wouldn't be reading this book and already into chapter five if you weren't this type of person. The question is, are you sharing in the right amount and in the right way? We may know very little about sharing. That is what we want to discuss in this chapter.

From a very young age we were taught that it is better to give than to receive. We were also taught that it is good to share, but probably the concept was not understood very well until we grew up. Then the context was understood only as situations involving tangible gifts or presents at Christmas time, birthdays and other special times. The context didn't have to do with sharing or giving of our talents and gifts in business, did it? That is what this chapter is about: sharing our gifts and talents effectively.

We agree that we want to share and that sharing is the right thing to do. We should also agree with the saying that " to those to whom much is given, much is asked." This means to share your gifts and talents abundantly and appropriately. But what does "sharing in the right way" mean? It means sharing with no ulterior motives. It means sharing without expecting something in return. It means sharing and not expecting praise and credit for what you have done. It means sharing so the receiving person is happy about what you have done and he or she still has his or her pride, dignity and motivation to personally succeed. It means sharing so that others will also want to share, not so much with you but with others. It means setting an example without anyone knowing you are setting an example. It means many times sharing without anyone even knowing who is the donor of your gifts.

Let me tell you about how God reminded me that I was sharing for the wrong reason. A few years ago my wife and I were driving along Midwestern Parkway in Wichita Falls and we saw a woman and two children by a stalled old car. They obviously needed help. I was feeling like a real Christian so I stopped to help. After about an hour of trying to jump the battery and get her car started, I decided it just wasn't going to start. So I offered to drive the woman and her children home, which was way on the other side of town. Again I was feeling proud of myself for doing this good deed. I was sharing my time and feeling good about it, but for the wrong reason. On the drive across town, the woman said to me that she would like to pay me for taking them home, and I replied that it wouldn't be necessary because I wasn't a taxi driver. She came right back with, "I know that and you sure aren't a mechanic either." This was a wonderful observation from her, but I really think it was a God-inspired message because I deserved it and I needed to have my sharing in the right way corrected.

I believe that this understanding of sharing in the right way makes it much easier to know where, when and how to share. Where to share has to do with where there is a need or an opportunity. Why else would you want to share? You want to help someone at work, help your company, help a friend, help an organization or help your family for a reason. The reason is that they can use your help and will be happier and more successful people or groups after you have shared with them in the right way. It might also simply be because they need a little more joy and happiness in their lives, and that is a good enough reason to share, isn't it?

It is important to believe in sharing information. Sharing information with your associates is a considerate thing to do, and generally it helps them do a better job and makes them feel like they are part of the team. As an example of this, we started circulating a report that showed daily order and revenue totals for everyone to see. Having this information so visible on a daily basis has helped to smooth out the flow of orders and shipments during the month. What gets measured and reported is what gets your attention. So why shouldn't the entire company be concerned about daily orders and shipments? It's what pays their salaries. Yours too!

If I ask you about lists again, how are you going to feel? Let's do it anyway. Take the list from chapter four where you listed your strengths. Now to this list add what you think your gifts are and also add your talents. I know it is difficult to separate these and you really don't have to, because all we are looking for is your own list for your own use. It will show a combination of your strengths (which we have already said shows where you like to spend your time), talents and gifts.

Your list could include some of these as an example:

Strengths:
    Good leadership
    Good motivation
    Ability to attract good people
    Good speaking ability
    Ability to make a good first impression
    High energy level
    Intelligence
    Good education
    Happiness

Talents:
    Empathy - understands people
    Understanding
    Ability to keep things in the proper perspective
    Good organization
    Ability to write effective reports
    Technical knowledge and skills

Gifts:
> Good listener
> Ability to make people feel at ease and express themselves
> Sense of humor
> Casual and balanced view of self
> Good communication
> Creativity
> Ability to understand what customers want

There will be others on your list.

If your list contains all of these, then I suggest you skip ahead to chapter 8 which is, "Don't Boast, Just Let It Happen"; read this chapter and then come back and start over with your list. Maybe it will change.

The next list should be one that includes needs for your company or your department in business and maybe a separate list for your family, friends and organizations. I would suggest you start with a small list involving those areas that are bothering you the most. First look to see if there are some needs that are not being met by anyone. There are jobs and positions in every organization and every company that nobody wants to do, but they have to be done. A good way to share your talents is to take one of these positions, such as membership chairman, and then do a great job of it. This is a win - win situation for you and for the organization and you definitely will not hurt any feelings. Is there an opportunity like this in your life, in business, that you can pursue? Any job worth doing is worth doing well.

Next list a few people who you think need help. Is there someone that you know who is hurting? Or someone who is going through a particularly difficult time? Many are in situations where they are really stressed and don't know how to cope with their environment. Do you know if these associates or friends recognize that they need help? Use your list to see if you have the gifts or talents to share what is needed. Probably you could help at least a few of your associates. I think it will be fairly clear to you where you should start.

How do you go about offering to share? Probably the best way is to ask for help. Ask someone to share with you. Ask one of the people you plan to share with for their help. There has to be some area where you could reasonably ask for their help. After you receive help, it will be fairly easy for you to reciprocate.

Sometimes a direct approach can be the best way to share either with an organization or with an associate. How about: "Could you use a little help from a friend?" You might want to even sing the words. Only kidding, unless you have a fine talent in that area.

Another good way is to have a third party make a suggestion that you might be willing to spend some time sharing your computer skills in making a PowerPoint presentation or whatever else you have to share. If the recipient of the favor doesn't feel right about asking, the third party friend can offer to do the asking. All this would achieve the results you want: you can share and the gift can be received.

You can get a great deal of personal satisfaction and have fun by sharing with those who don't expect it or by doing more than is expected. If someone in need asks for bread, give them cake. If customers ask for bread or expect bread from you, give them cake. To me it is really fun when traveling in areas where you are expected to negotiate prices to agree on a price and then to pay more than the negotiated price. One example was negotiating a price for jewelry in Cancun, Mexico. After fun discussions with the store owner we agreed on a price of $20.00 for a silver bracelet. Then I told him I wanted to pay $25.00. His surprise and what followed was worth more than $5.00. I tell you when you share like this, the relationship becomes entirely different and there will be sharing both ways. Try it sometime.

Jim Coghlin, CEO of Coghlin Companies, shared with me that his favorite focus in life is "The Joy is in the Giving." He is very proactive when he senses that people are "hurting" and usually this hurt is caused by some type of an illness that either they are experiencing or someone dear to them is experiencing. He says, "It is absolutely amazing what can happen when you extend a helping hand to someone in need. Believe me, there is no better feeling than reaching out to someone and that act enables them to enhance their life's journey."

I believe if you truly want to share in the right way and there are needs for your gifts and talents, which of course there are, you will know the right way to share. Let your subconscious mind work on the challenge. You will probably get some other special help.

In summary, work on all these sharing actions "In the right way":
- Share with someone who is hurting
- Share with someone who needs your gifts and talents
- Share with someone who doesn't expect it
- Share joy and happiness every day
- Share some good humor
- Share more than what is expected - give them cake
- Share in business and in life
- Share in a Christian way

Make your mother proud!

Priorities & Actions
Strengths, Talents & Gifts

Strengths, Talents & Gifts	Business needs	Personal needs	Those That Are in Need of Help	How Can I Help?

Priorities & Actions
How I Spend My Time in Business

Date	Length of time	Activity	Name	Name	Name	Name	Others

Look up and be ready to receive sunshine in your life today. There is so much to be seen by looking upward in a receptive and positive way

Chapter Six – The Second Priority
Family

We don't have to go through a guessing game here because I have already told you the second priority is family. After love how could the second priority be anything other than family and, as we said back in the love chapter, they go together!

In the news lately there have been articles about grandparents going to court so that they can have the right to see their grandchildren. What is wrong with those families and their priorities? If the first priority is love and the second is family, what in the world went wrong? Why can't the grandparents see their own grandchildren? Who is the loser here? Everyone — the parents, the grandparents and most of all the little grandchildren - and probably many others including friends and other family members. What can be done about fractured families? Is there an answer? I believe there has to be some good way to bring these families back together again. There just has to be for those that should be together.

There are certain circumstances where time and space may be essential for reasonable healing and this should be respected. In these cases the need for having patience and understanding should be clear. Wait for the right time.

Maybe this is an extreme case, but we hear about many families who haven't seen each other in years. What happened to cause the long separation? If your family is one of these, I would suggest that you do whatever is possible to find the right answer and take the right actions to get the family back together again. Some suggestions in this book might help.

This book is about using actions and having the right priorities that will help you be successful in business and in life. You might say, "How does this family priority fit in with being successful in business?" The answer is that you cannot be truly happy and successful in business if you are not happy at home with your family. The reverse is also true. Earlier in the book we asked if it is possible to be successful in both business and life, and we said we would discuss this later, and we will. The two should go together.

Hopefully - and most likely - you are not in a critical family situation, but do you know someone who is hurting in this way? Your family probably is one where grandparents are always welcome and you know where all your family members are and what they are doing. Good for you and your family; but is the family in real life actually your number two priority? Think about this. Think about this day, this week and this month. What have you done with your time, your gifts, your talents and your love? How much of your time and your gifts have been spent on family? These questions are not meant to make you feel guilty; they are to help you put your values in the right perspective so you can understand where you are today.

Let's decide first of all who the family is. There are two general families that we will be discussing in this chapter. The first is your own family and the other your business family. The most important is of course your own family, but we want you to understand that we also have a business family.

Who is your own family? It is up to you to decide how large this family should be. It should be at least you, your spouse, your children (if you have children), your parents and your spouse's parents. Who is missing? Let me add one. You have an earthly father and you have a heavenly father. He should be included in your family. You might want to include brothers and sisters, cousins and so forth. That is up to you. This family should be a high priority in your life.

While traveling in Mexico and South America these last two years I have been very impressed with the importance of the family to our Latin America neighbors. They love each other and they spend time together regularly. Big family dinners on Sunday and usually one other day during the week are common. I think they have a handle on their priorities, at least as far as the family is concerned.

Now back to the question about how much time you spend with your family. Do you really know? I would like to suggest that you use a new form to help you better understand just how you are spending your time. This will be a form for you and only you, so you might as well be honest about it. It is a good idea to determine how much time you spend with family, isn't it? Don't you want to know? Time management is important to all of us because we just never seem to have enough time to do all that we want to do. That is why priorities are so important to being successful in business and in life. Because we have so little time, we need to know how we are spending it.

This form should be detailed enough so it will show you, after a month, just how you spent your time, including how much was spent with each family member and what you did together. It will also show just how much time was spent doing business things and how much time was spent doing your own things. There should be a form for your own family and a form for your business family. You really should complete both of them. Use the forms at the end of the chapter or make your own.

The business family is the group of business associates that you are with on a regular basis. You know who they are and it is up to you to decide how small or large this family list will be. It will be interesting and important to see how you are spending your time during your business hours. Are you spending the right amount of time with each of your business family members?

There are some companies that are now requiring their managers to spend a certain amount of time each week going to their children's activities. They actually have to have a plan and submit it to their supervisor each week showing what they plan to do and what they did the previous week. This is like a salesman's call plan. Why are companies doing this? They say their managers are getting burned out with all the pressure, and stress is affecting their health and performance. This is true, but I would say the problem is caused by not having the right priorities. Why do you have to have a "call plan" to spend time with your family? Why do you have to have your boss tell you to go to Billy's baseball game? If the company isn't making you spend so much time away from your family, who is? Is it really you who needs to evaluate your priorities? If this is the case, using these forms will at least show you how far off the mark you are. Then it is up to you to do something about it!

You know you should plan the work and then work the plan. You just don't start out working on a project without having a plan. Planning is so important to a successful project. Why not put the same importance on planning for the family as is done in business? Plan to enjoy the family and make it happen. Family is after all the number two priority and it deserves your best planning efforts.

Talk to your company about the need and importance of this priority for you and for all employees. See if the company can't promote a policy where parents are encouraged to take part in their children's activities that take place during working hours. Remember that working hours now commonly include evenings and weekends. We need to take these extended hours into account for all employees. Surely there can be a way to make up the few hours that you spent watching your daughter in the school play. You know you should not miss her performance, and her seeing you there is a memory that she will not forget. What few hours at work could possibly be as important as this sharing, loving experience?

It might be a good idea to make up similar forms and give them to your family members and ask them to fill them out for themselves. Do they have enough time for you and do they seem to have the right priorities? I think about the song "Cat's In The Cradle" by Harry Chapin and Sandy Chapin, in which the son is always asking the father to play catch or spend time with him and he doesn't have time to do it. Then, later in life, the father wants to do things with his grown son, but the son doesn't have time for him. Both say, "maybe later" and "we'll have a good time then!" But maybe later is too late. It doesn't have to be too late for you to make sure your number one and number two priorities are love and family.

There is another song, "Busy Man," sung by Billy Ray Cyrus, written by Bob Regan and George Teren, that is similar. The son, the daughter and the wife all want to spend time with the father, but he says he can't now because he's a "busy man." In this song the father is asked if he ever saw a tombstone that says, "If only I'd spent more time at work." After hearing this question, he recognizes the need for new priorities and he changes. Two songs, same situation, but with different endings. Only one ends happily. Discovering and accepting the right priorities is the difference. These are only songs, right? Wouldn't happen in real life. Really? Maybe it would be good to listen to these songs again.

In every family at some time or other there are issues that are extremely hard to deal with in a loving way. This quite often has to do with giving "tough love." It is important to recognize these times and take actions that are right for the family. This can be done while still keeping the right priorities and taking the right actions that we are discussing in this book. This situation might require making some sacrifices, but they aren't real sacrifices if they are being done out of love.

Each day why not think about each family member? Take a few minutes to think about where family members are, what they are doing, what their immediate needs and problems are, and what their joys and successes are. Then think how I can be a part of this. How can I share? Should I call or should I go see them? My answer to that is always "Yes." If there is ever a question of doing something or not, just do it. Gretchen and I started thinking this way some years ago. It really had to do with visiting someone at home after her husband died and we didn't know whether we should go see her or not. We did it and it was the right thing to do. After that we have always said if there is a question of whether or not to do something, do it. We have never regretted the decision and I'm sure this will be the case with you too, even more so if it is about doing something with or for your family.

Do the same for your business family. Think about each one each day. Treat business associates like family.

When you are thinking about family members, consider what each would like to do with you. Don't think, "What would I like to do with them?" Maybe those preferences will be the same, but you should be thinking of others first and what would make them the happiest. What would the family most like to do as a family? Remember the family is made up of men and women and perhaps boys and girls so consider all of the family and the differences in their interests and abilities. Plan to enjoy the family!

Now is the time to:
- Do whatever is necessary to fix family problems
- Bring the family back together
- Learn from your time forms where you are spending your time
- Decide how this will be different in the future
- Talk to your company about the family priority
- Think about each family member each day
- Consider what would they like to do with you - with the family
- Ask yourself who in the family needs my help today

Priorities & Actions
How I Spend My Time with My Family

Date	Length of time	Activity	Name	Name	Name	Name	Others

Priorities & Actions
How I Spend My Time in Business

Date	Length of time	Activity	Name	Name	Name	Name	Others

Everyone has special gifts, talents and interests. It is okay not to have all of them because we need to share and accept sharing from others. Use the help!

Chapter Seven – Action Number Four
Give Thanks for Priorities & Actions

You might be thinking that action number one was to give thanks. It was, but this is different. This is my turn to give thanks and then maybe for you to also give thanks and share in a different way.

It would not be right to be writing this book without giving thanks for the help I have received in learning of the ten actions and the five priorities and for the help in the actual writing of the book. Remember that earlier I said it was we who are writing this book and went on to explain that I believe we always have help in whatever we do. Help can come in many ways. There is good help and unfortunately sometimes bad help. Help from God can only be good help and I know I have received only good help with *Time Out...It's Your Call*. The help came from God, who shared with me the five priorities and ten actions.

There is a risk that as you read this book and receive all the advice, suggestions and instructions, you might think, "It is easy to give advice, but much more difficult to follow it. Does the author actually do all this himself?" This would be a good question and a good observation on your part. In fact, I would ask you to please think of this book as one with more than one author. I could not have conceived priorities and actions alone and couldn't have written the book without God's help. So be open and think of the messages, not about who wrote the book. That really doesn't matter. What matters is that there are some messages that are worthwhile for helping you become more successful in business and life. Your success is what counts.

To partially answer the questions about the author, let me say that, yes, I feel I have been successful in business and in my personal life. Concerning all the advice and suggestions in the book, I would say that some come from personal experiences and others from personal observations. See how many of these thoughts make sense to you and how many new ones you find from your own experiences and observations.

We know there is much asked of you and there are many demands on your time so it is probably unrealistic to think that you would follow all of these suggestions at once. So far there are many things to think about in the first six chapters discussing three actions and two priorities and quite a number of lists to complete. Should you do all of them at once as you read through the book? That is up to you. Some will be more beneficial than others for you to start on, you know what your most important needs are. I would, however, suggest doing at least a little with each one because in that way you will be able to quickly identify how important it is for you. Each list is not intended to be one that you complete in one sitting. They all should be working documents that you add to and modify as you grow with these actions and priorities in your own life and your own business relationships.

Next I would again ask you to do something. Think about how you can become involved with *Time Out...It's Your Call* and how you might give thanks and share with others from your own experiences. You have them! We hope there will be a follow-up book to this one where we take the experiences from our readers and share them. Would you like to be a part of this?

I would like to give an example of this sharing. Dr. John Muir is a good friend who agreed to read *Time Out...It's Your Call* in the manuscript form to help with thoughts on religious concepts. Here is one of John's contributions and what he had to say:

> For whatever it's worth I want to make a statement about my management style. You can consider it the first response to your request for feedback from the book. Use it any way you want to or not at all!
>
> My management style is ably stated by the German philosopher, playwright, Goethe (1749-1832) who wrote, 'If you merely accept a person as you find them, you add nothing to their life, but if you treat that person as if they had already become what they have the potential to become, then you help to enable them to fulfill their potential.' I have been amazed at the productive response of persons who were treated with a new sense of respect. The usual response was a striving on the part of the person to be worthy of this new found respect.

Isn't this a wonderful message? How many more of these valuable contributions could come from you and others? This is why I am asking for you to think about your experiences and messages that you have similar to John's. It is early in the book so you have time to consider sharing thoughts as you continue reading *Time Out...It's Your Call*.

If you agree that these experiences and messages will be valuable as a follow-up book, please consider doing the following:

- Send your unique experiences that have helped you to become successful in business and/or life. What are they?
- Send your experiences where God has been directly involved in helping you or someone close to you.
- When you asked God directly for help, how has he answered your prayer? Please share that with us.
- Do you have questions or have a particular problem that you would like to send where possibly others might be able to provide some help? This information of course would be confidential. Your questions should have to do with your being successful in business or life. We can put your question or problem on our web site and others can give answers or comments from their own experiences that might be helpful.

For the first three experiences listed above, please also send your approval for us to use your message or your story in a future book and give permission to use your name and hometown. I know there is the feeling that when good things happen to you, your family or your business, you want to share them, but not in a boastful way. Please send them in to me and trust me to share them with others so that it will not be embarrassing to you or presented in a boastful way.

You can e-mail this information to our web site at www.bridgmantimeout.com or send to:

>Bridgman Consulting
>3610 Glenwood
>Wichita Falls, Texas 76308

Action Number Four

You can make notes to yourself as you read through the book and when you feel so motivated, send them to the above address or web site. Thanks for doing this.

Now, on to the next chapter.

Priorities & Actions
Experiences I Would Like to Share

	Your Approval to Print Experience Signature: Date:										
Experiences I Would Like to Share											

Action Number Four

Priorities & Actions
Questions That I Would Like to Ask

Comments

Questions That I Would Like to Ask

Smile – you're on God's candid camera! Think about how you are performing. Are you performing up to your capabilities considering your strengths, talents and gifts?

Chapter Eight – Action Number Five
Don't Boast, Just Let It Happen

Two years ago we were on a cruise and had the wonderful experience of spending three days in Israel. We took advantage of the time there to go on three different full-day tours and all three had great tour guides.

One day our tour guide handed my wife Gretchen a card and asked her if she wouldn't mind reading it aloud for the whole bus to hear when we came to a certain location. He was such an interesting and nice guy that she really couldn't say no. Well, when we came to that location, where Jesus preached his Sermon on the Mount, he asked Gretchen to read the Beatitudes. The experience was beautiful. Can you imagine the feelings we had that day being where Jesus walked and where he taught so many? And to hear my dear wife read the Beatitudes was wonderful. I'll never forget it.

I think the Beatitudes fit in here so well because we are in the chapter in which we are being told that the next action is "don't boast, just let it happen." Let's read them again from Matthew 5:3 - 12.

- Blessed are the poor in spirit, for theirs is the Kingdom of Heaven.
- Blessed are they that mourn, for they shall be comforted.

- Blessed are the meek, for they shall inherit the earth.
- Blessed are they which do hunger and thirst after righteousness, for they shall be filled.
- Blessed are the merciful, for they shall obtain mercy.
- Blessed are the pure in heart, for they shall see God.
- Blessed are the peacemakers, for they shall be called the children of God.
- Blessed are they which are persecuted for righteousness sake, for theirs is the kingdom of heaven.
- Blessed are you when people revile you and persecute you and utter all kinds of evil against you falsely on my account.
- Rejoice, and be glad, for your reward is great in heaven, for in the same way they persecuted the prophets who were before you.

How may we be successful in business and in life? Just read the Beatitudes again and see how this point of view today is still so right for dealing with associates and others in business and life.

To those that much is given, much is asked. How can we give thanks, use the help and share in the right way to make these Beatitudes alive and well today in our quest for success in business and in life? Definitely it is not by being boastful in words or actions.

I think "Don't boast, just let it happen" has to do with doing less talking and doing way more listening to your family, your customers and your business associates. It's very difficult to boast when listening and caring about what someone is telling you. How much time each day do you spend really listening to what others are saying? I'm not going to ask you to make a list here, but think about it. Are you more of a listener or more of a talker? Do others think you might be boastful, sometimes?

Boasting doesn't do anything positive or productive, and there is no question that it turns people off. Action is what is positive, not talking about action. Peter Janson, when he was president of ABB in the United States, had as a goal to have ABB become known as an incredibly customer-focused company experiencing profitable growth. This goal is really profound, because you start trying to picture what an incredibly customer-focused company really is. Not just good or very good but incredibly good. Then when you take on this vision and try to make it happen in your own company, you don't go out to your customers and say, "We are incredibly customer-focused" or "We plan to be incredibly customer-focused." You achieve the goal in a different way. You don't boast.

You go to customers and listen to their needs and the ideas they have as to how you can help them to become more successful. Then you develop actions so you can become incredibly customer-focused for them, not for you. So talking about being incredibly customer-focused is internal. Your actions and performance with your customers, not your words, will show that you are indeed incredibly customer-focused.

At ABB Control we promoted both externally and internally the mission statement Customer First...Quality Always, and added internally only the goal of being recognized as an incredibly customer-focused company. You should be known by your actions and deeds not by your words.

It is important to have confidence and to be yourself, and both can be achieved without boasting. Some years ago Gretchen and I wrote "Some Advice for the Graduating Senior," and I would like to share parts of this with you because I think it is appropriate for other situations in business and life, not just for the senior preparing to interview for a job. See if these suggestions might also be useful for anyone you know or for other situations.

Some Advice for the Graduating Senior

There is much that can be shared with the senior as he or she begins interviewing companies on or off campus. Take the time to learn from others who have successfully interviewed and found the right job for them. There are some ideas that we would like to share with you that you might want to think about prior to beginning this exciting and important part of your college career.

- Be yourself. The company is looking to interview the real you.
- Be prepared. Be early and mentally and physically prepared for this experience.
- Relax.
- Enjoy yourself. Think about this goal in advance and tell yourself, "I am going to have a good time today."
- Look and feel good and professional. You know what this means.
- Learn about the company you are interviewing - use the Internet. There might be some interesting new developments, acquisitions or large orders that you could discuss.
- The interview is for you too. You know you are interviewing the company also - it is a two-way process.
- Think about the questions that might be asked in a first interview and the answers that would be most appropriate for the company you are interviewing.

Some additional general hints:

- Some interviewers try to get students to argue. If for some reason you don't agree with what the interviewer is saying, don't make a big deal of it. He might be testing you. Respect his position.

- Don't worry about pauses in the conversation. They seem to be much longer than they really are. Also, remember it is the interviewer's responsibility to carry the conversation, not yours.

- Smile, relax, have a natural sense of humor; do not be silly and certainly never use any profanity or needless reference to partying, drinking or sex. Present yourself at your best.

- Interviewers look at posture. Look the interviewer straight in the eye, and leave with a firm handshake. Look the interviewer in the eye when you give him or her the firm handshake and say thanks.

- Look at interviewing as a fun and exciting experience. The worst thing that they could do to you in an interview would be to shoot you! Obviously only kidding. The worst thing that could happen is that you simply don't get a job offer. Everything else is positive.

- There is absolutely nothing wrong with being a little nervous; some anxiety is natural. The interviewer might even be a little nervous about talking to you.

I especially want to emphasize the importance of not arguing with your boss or an associate or a family member in general, especially about something that really isn't very important. Unfortunately I see this happen all too often. People argue and get upset about little things. Don't do it. Simply just don't do it. Nobody wins and everyone loses in one way or another. It doesn't make sense to win the battle and lose the war. You know arguing is a form of boasting because it is saying I am right and you are wrong or I know more than you do and I'm going to let you know how much I really know. If you have to disagree, do it in private, never with others around or when others can hear. Do it face to face not in an e-mail or a voice mail. Remember good news can be shared by any means of communications, but bad news or anything that would be controversial should be done only face to face.

Don't boast or raise yourself up and in so doing lower someone else. Support and build up your family members, your friends and your business associates. Why should people ever say anything that would make a friend, associate or someone from their own family feel bad or look bad in public or in private. What could possibly be gained by doing that?

Remember the Golden Rule from Matthew 7:12: "In everything do to others as you would have them do to you; for this is the law and the prophets."

Just be yourself, the self that you like and others like too. Don't boast, just let it happen!

Slow down, you're going too fast. Take time to enjoy your family, friends and business associates. you earned the blessing of sharing and they deserve it.

Chapter Nine – Priority Number Three
Joy

After love and family the next priority is joy. What is "joy" and what does it mean? Joy, like wisdom, is a gift from God. For our purposes, here, joy means great happiness. It is more than just happiness; it is great happiness. In this definition we need to be clear that we understand that happiness comes from doing the right things. We don't go out and plan to obtain happiness or great happiness. We go out to do the right things and from these intentions we obtain happiness. Happiness is a by-product of taking the right actions and having the right priorities.

Let's just take a few minutes and think about joy and our lives. How much joy do we experience each day, each week, or however often it happens? Is there enough joy so that we are thought of as joyful people? Do you feel like a joyful person? Are you basically a joyful person and how much of the time is this so? Do you help others to be joyful? Can you have joy in business?

I think we don't have enough joy in our lives though this is the third priority after love and family. We should get great joy from our family through sharing our love and receiving love from those we care about. But that just doesn't happen often enough. We get into business and personal ruts. We keep doing the same things over and over and doing them without joy or without the right feeling about ourselves and others. It is not a joyful way to be living and it is not the way to be successful in business and in life. There should to be joy in whatever we do.

Jim Truba is a good friend of mine and a business associate. When I joined Asea many years ago, we hired Jim to be our rep in Detroit. He is extremely creative and successful and has a way of getting customers to want to do business with him. As an example, one time when we were both working for Cutler-Hammer in Detroit, we made a presentation to General Motors on C-H's new line of limit switches. Jim painted the limit switch red, white and blue and for the lever he made a small American flag. He then recited the Gettysburg Address, which he changed to be a sales pitch for limit switches. During this recitation, three of us hummed the Battle Hymn of the Republic in the background. After he finished he received a standing ovation from the GM engineers. This reaction was almost unheard of. We also received approval to be added to their specifications. I should also add that it was an excellent limit switch and deserved to be on their specifications.

Jim was a joyful person doing joyful things in business. Those around Jim shared this joy. He was doing the right things at the right time in his life.

A few years later Jim decided he didn't want to be a manufacturer's rep any longer, and we offered him a job as our Midwest regional manager. He accepted this job, but while the two of us were discussing this new association it occurred to me that there was no joy in this decision. I asked Jim if he was really happy about this decision and after a few minutes of thought he said no. It was clear that this wasn't going to be the right thing to do. So together we decided that Jim should do something that would make him happy. There needed to be joy in his decision. Jim finally merged his rep business with another rep firm in Detroit and, as the story goes, everyone lived happily ever after.

This is an example that I think shows how easy it is to make decisions that are not joyful, and decisions that can dramatically affect our lives. With important decisions like this in business or in life, shouldn't we ask these questions: "How much joy will there be for me and my family with this decision? How much joy will I be able to share with my business associates? Am I doing the right things?"

At this very time I am involved in a business opportunity that has to do with joy and has to do with priorities. I have decided to share this with you and write about it as it progresses. It has to do with a company we are trying to acquire that has two owners who are about ready to sell, but probably aren't quite ready to accept retirement. It is a common dilemma. Our competitor has a head start on this acquisition and we are trying to catch up. You could say we are the underdog.

In our first meeting with one of the owners, he said it was about time for him to sell the company and then he would go home and probably die. Right away I said to him, "Don't do that! It is your company and you can do whatever you want to do with it, but don't do something that will make you unhappy. There are many options; stay with the company, become a consultant, sell part of the business, but being unhappy should not be an option." He had worked too hard and too long to just give up his very successful company and go home. We all think he appreciated this advice and our sincere concern for him.

To help the owners understand just what selling their company really means, we made up a list of what we thought the priorities for them should be. We asked them to make up their own list, but gave them ours just to help them get started. Here is the list:

> In business as in life there is an important difference between following your priorities and accepting a decision that just isn't right for any number of reasons. My feeling is that you should always first consider your priorities and act on these in an order of the most important priorities first and then continuing down the list until you cover all the ones that are most appropriate for the decision to be made.
>
> This is our list of priorities to share with the owners:
>
> #1. The satisfaction of the owners is primary. Can they get a fair price for their company that properly rewards them for their success and all the years and energy they put into their company?
>
> #2. The acceptance and respect of the families of the owners is second. Can they sell the company and sell it to a company that leaves the families with good feelings and closeness?
>
> #3. The employees of the company would probably be next. Will the purchasing company be a good company for the employees to work for and will the company "protect" the key employees that the owners especially want to take care of?
>
> #4. The community might be next. How will the new company be received in the community and will

the company keep its present location and grow with it in the local community?

#5. Customers are of course important. Will the acquiring company demand the continuation of customer care and support for the existing reps and customers?

#6. The personnel of the acquiring company should be a fairly high priority. It is important that there is trust and confidence between the management of both companies and they feel they can easily and openly work together.

#7. The success of the company in future years is also important. The owners put a great deal of themselves into this company and it is important that they would know the acquiring company is very much committed to the success and future growth of their company.

#8. Would the owners want to be involved at all in a consulting role or in any way? Is there the possibility that they would so desire to do this either now or in the future?

#9. How will this acquisition be perceived in their industry?

#10. How will the owners feel about their decision in one year, two years and five years? How important is this decision now — meaning selecting the best company to sell to? It probably is extremely important.

This would be my top 10, but what is important is what are their top 10 priorities and whether they can follow them.

I think this analysis has to do with joy. The owners should be able to sell their company and move into a different stage in their lives with great happiness because they did the right things - with joy.

Our strategy is now to meet again with the owners and the question comes up as to who from our company should attend the meeting? Remember earlier I said that if there is a question of doing something or not, just do it! In line with practicing what you preach, the answer as to whether or not I should attend this meeting is yes, just do it. Speaking of "just do it" I should add that I was excited to see Nike a few years ago when they started using this saying in their advertising - "Just do it." Obviously Nike didn't get this from me, but I have been using this saying for a very long time and appreciated seeing it often on TV. Now I say "go for it!"

After a meeting like this there could be one of the following conclusions depending on if you attended or not:

- I'm glad I was in the meeting. I was able to make some contributions that were necessary at the time.
- The meeting wasn't successful; maybe I should have attended.
- The meeting would have been successful with or without my being there.
- Either with success or not, there will be no second guessing if you're there.

If you analyze what the conclusions about the meeting might be, it is then clear what action should be taken. Go for it!

If you take the time to think about whether you should do something or not, you should do it, or why else would you have even spent the time thinking about it in the first place? Go for it. Also, why not add a little joy to the meeting?

This possible acquisition example is one that is happening in real time and in real life to show the importance of joy, our third priority. If you look at the priorities we listed for this company, the first was joy, the second was family, and joy and love of the business were in all of them in one way or another.

This example is also about selling (promoting and persuading). Anything worthwhile requires and deserves attention. Just because you have a good idea or are right doesn't mean that everyone else will appreciate that it is a good idea or understand that it is right. Everything requires some degree of selling and no one is ever above selling what is a good idea or what is right. Look at how much positive promoting and persuading the Disciples had to do even with such a powerful message.

Just think how much more meaningful your life would be if there was more joy in it. Just also think how much more joyful life would be for your family, friends and business associates if you were more of a joyful person. Is the quest for joy important enough to do something about it? How could you get more joy into your life if you really wanted to? Do you know the answers to this? Would you share them with me? You have my address and e-mail address, so why not share them with me. I think joy is very important and probably not many people know what to do to feel joyful.

Let me list a few other ideas here. First, I would suggest you use a new form titled, "Things I Like To Do That Bring Me Joy." Spend some time thinking about this and then start writing them down. It might not be easy at first, but you can do it. Then the next form should be, "Things I Like To Do That Bring Joy To Others." There should also be a column that says "Why." Why does this bring you or others joy? If you are bringing joy to someone else, are you also bringing joy to yourself at the same time? The third and last form to use here is, "Ways That I Will Use Joy In Business And Life." Notice the form has a date column and a comments column to record the results of your sharing joys.

Take your time with this.

In the Bible, "Joy" occurs 165 times in 155 verses, and "Joyful" occurs 25 times in 25 verses. Quality and quantity in this instance mean a lot. A few of them are included here:

- But the angel said to them, 'Do not be afraid; for see- I am bringing you good news of great joy for all the people:.' (Luke 2:10)
- I have said these things to you so that my joy may be in you and that your joy may be complete. (John 15:11)
- You have shown me the paths that lead to life, and your presence will fill me with joy. (Acts 2:28)
- So there was great joy in that city. (Acts 8:8)
- And the disciples were filled with joy, and with the Holy Spirit. (Acts 13:52)
- And not only so, but we also joy in God through our Lord Jesus Christ, by who we have now received the atonement. (Romans 5:11)
- May God, the source of hope, fill you with all joy and peace by means of your faith in him, so that your hope will continue to grow by the power of the Holy Spirit. (Romans 15:13)

- And so I will come to you full of joy, if it is God's will, and enjoy a refreshing visit with you. (Romans 15:32)
- "Indeed, you are our pride and joy!" (I Thessalonians 2:20)

It seems clear that great joy can come first from God and then from the first two priorities, love and family. "Praise God with shouts of joy, all people!" (Psalms 66:1)

Priorities & Actions
Things I Like To Do That Bring Me Joy

Why

Acitivity

Priority Number Three

Priorities & Actions
Things I Like To Do That Bring Joy to Others

Why

Acitivity

Priorities & Actions
Ways That I Will Use Joy in Business & Life

Why

Acitivity

Remember to use reason, logic and common sense, especially in how you communicate with your friends, family and associates. Be considerate today, tomorrow and always!

Chapter Ten – Action Number Six
Be Grateful

We have so far discussed five actions and three priorities. The next action is "Be Grateful."

I believe that for us to become successful, or more successful, in business and life, we must have a grateful frame of mind or attitude. A positive person is grateful for being alive and being a part of all that is happening and can happen in business and in life. Gratitude enables us to take advantage of the opportunities that are available to us. It empowers us with optimism and creativity that shows to all around.

The grateful person knows that for whatever reason, he or she has found favor with God and He is continually providing blessings every day. It is exciting to see what that favor will mean each new day. Are you grateful? If not, action number six should become a goal: become a grateful person.

I am not going to talk about the need to be grateful and the benefits of being grateful. This chapter about being grateful is just to read and enjoy because that is what being grateful is about. You should enjoy the feelings and personal satisfaction of this wonderful state of mind and have a positive attitude. A beautiful day should provide you with an untold number of ways you can use the actions we have already discussed. Have you set aside some time for reflection today? If not, why not? What is more important right now than contemplating what you know you can do in the future?

This feeling made me think about an excerpt I just read from *A Charge To Keep*, written by George W. Bush. I would like to share some of this with you because I believe it helps to show the real George Bush and his feeling of being grateful, which to me comes through loud and clear.

> "Actually, the seeds of my decision had been planted the year before, by the Reverend Billy Graham. He visited my family for a summer weekend in Maine. I saw him preach at the small summer church, St. Ann's by the Sea. We all had lunch on the patio overlooking the ocean. One evening my dad asked Billy to answer questions from a big group of family gathered for the weekend. He sat by the fire and talked. And what he said sparked a change in my heart. I don't remember the exact words. It was more the power of his example. The Lord was so clearly reflected in his gentle and loving demeanor.
>
> The next day we walked and talked at Walker's Point, and I knew I was in the presence of a great man. He was like a magnet; I felt drawn to seek something different. He didn't lecture or admonish; he shared warmth and concern. Billy Graham didn't make you feel guilty; he made you feel loved.
>
> Over the course of that weekend, Reverend Graham planted a mustard seed in my soul, a seed that grew over the next year. He led me to the path, and I began walking. And it was the beginning of a change in

my life. I had always been a religious person, had regularly attended church, even taught Sunday school and served as an altar boy. But that weekend my faith took on a new meaning. It was the beginning of a new walk where I would recommit my heart to Jesus Christ.

I was humbled to learn that God sent His Son to die for a sinner like me. I was comforted to know that through the Son, I could find God's amazing grace, a grace that crosses every border, every barrier and is open to everyone. Through the love of Christ's life, I could understand the life-changing powers of faith."

I know this is the kind of man we want as our president leading our country and being an example for our young people. This excerpt is meaningful for us and we should appreciate that George Bush shared his thoughts with us.

I have at times been criticized by my business associates as being too much of an optimist and always trying to see the best in our employees. The criticism was meant to be constructive and was given in a good way because they felt I was always thinking that the glass was half full and not half empty. Do you know what I mean here? If I was thinking about it being half empty, I would be looking for ways to fill it up so to speak, rather than spending time looking for ways to use this half full glass. I know there has to be a balance, but believe me, the balance can and will come from others who seem to always look at the glass and see it as half empty. "We have a serious problem because the glass is almost empty," they say. This pessimism can be experienced almost every day. The world needs full-time optimists.

Time spent with a pessimist seems to beat you down and depress you, while an optimist makes you feel energetic, constructive, creative. Optimism usually comes from a grateful person.

One of the many learning experiences I've had occurred when I was marketing manager for another company. We had an inside sales person whom our sales people referred to as Mr. No. He really was Mr. No because whenever he was asked something his first reply was "No." How do you change a real Mr. No to a Mr. Yes? I honestly don't know if you can. We had another who hated to be bothered by customers calling in if he was busy. With this company our sales people advised our customers that if they called in for customer service and a man answered to just hang up and call back later. How customer-focused do you think these two were? I tried giving Dale Carnegie's *How to Win Friends and Influence People* and Norman Vincent Peale's *The Power of Positive Thinking* to these employees, but it really didn't help. What I learned from this experience was to take the offensive and try to hire "yes" thinking people and create an atmosphere where positive thinking is the norm, not the exception.

At ABB Control we were fortunate in that we could create our own atmosphere and hire mostly all our own people. So we started with one of our internal mission statements that read: "Just say yes!" In other words, when a customer would ask us to do something, we would have the positive mental attitude of saying "yes" first, and then deciding how we would do it and what would be required of the customer. It works. There are those whom you know who first look at a situation or an opportunity and study all the reasons why it won't work or what can go wrong or what isn't right about it. If they go through this list of ten negative things, there just isn't time or energy to then look at the positives. It's too late then. Whereas if you first look at all the good things and decide you want to make something happen, it probably will, and I believe you will do a better job of putting the negatives in the right perspective. This is a very real situation that I'm sure you have experienced, and it all starts and stops because of being led by a grateful person with a positive attitude, or the other way around.

Being grateful in life makes me think of the times when I see parents and grandparents with children meeting each other in airports. With so many there is such love and happiness shown. You can feel the power of their love and it is wonderful.

But how about when you see a parent being really mean to a son or daughter and telling the child how bad the child is and doing it in public. You know what I mean. Parents say some really cruel things to these little ones and in front of other people. No wonder some of these little ones grow up with problems and low self esteem. What kind of parents do you think they will be? When you see this behavior it makes you want to pick up the little one, give a hug and say it is okay: God loves you. You know this reassurance sometimes also needs to be done in business. Good caring management is about picking up employees, giving them a hug and telling them that they are okay. Here I mean verbal hugs. Those who can do this are being grateful, successful managers because of the results they get and the personal satisfaction that comes from being a grateful person.

This grateful and positive attitude also has to do with winning in business and in life. If you have this kind of attitude and really plan to win in whatever it is, you can do it. Let's say the goal is to get a large order or win a new account. If from the beginning all planning and strategy is based on winning, the outcome will be positive and energies will be spent on doing what is necessary to win. We try to answer these questions:

- Do we want to win this order or account?
- Do we deserve to win?
- Do we have the right products?
- Do they know our product features and our capabilities?
- Do they have a good reason to change suppliers?
- Do we have an internal champion to sell for us?
- If we were the customer would we buy from us?
- What can we do better than the competition?
- They are asking for bread; how can we give them cake?
- Do we know the decision-makers and who supports their decisions?

All of these are positive questions geared to help us win, not lose. Then with these questions answered it is up to the team to make sure the customer knows that we are a grateful, caring company.

Winners win. When going after an order or an account, there is only one ribbon that you want: first place!

I am grateful for a number of opportunities that seemed to happen at the right time. Let me tell you about a few of them. One day we were discussing the need to have a creative, talented and experienced person do our literature and advertising. We thought it might be somewhat difficult to find someone like that in Wichita Falls, Texas. As we were talking the receptionist interrupted our meeting to tell us there was a young man in the lobby who wanted to interview for a job. He was just getting out of the Air Force and his major in college was advertising. It was Steve Chase, who was absolutely perfect for the job, and still is our Manager of Marketing Services.

Another time our management team told me in a nice and tactful way that we had grown to the size where we needed a full-time sales manager. They meant I should be the president and not the president and sales manager. I agreed with them even though I hated to give up the sales involvement. That very day I got a call from an old friend, Pat Hogan from Lansing, Michigan, who told me he was leaving the company there and wondered if I knew of any openings in our industry. It was as if he had been in our meeting, just waiting to talk to me about this position. Pat became our first VP of Sales and Marketing and just recently became the President of ABB Control after I became Group Vice President for the Americas. Both of these were great coincidences. Or were they? Other people in our company have been available at the right time for us and for their personal situations. Is it a coincidence, or luck, or what?

I am grateful for all the good people who have joined our company and made it the success that it is. I thank God for his help in attracting these people.

Percy Barnevik was president of Asea when I joined the company. In fact he hired me to try to grow the control business in the U.S. I would like to use Percy as an example here because of the tremendous success he has had and the influence he has had on ABB and its many employees. Besides being very intelligent, he is a positive thinker with great vision, and I believe he is a very grateful person as well.

We struggled for the first few years during our start up in the United States, but Percy stood behind us, encouraging us and personally showing his interest and support for what we were doing. He was positive and he had the vision to see that the business would work. I think others in his position might not have stood firm. So I am grateful to Percy, and I learned a great deal from him.

Percy was then the driving force behind the merger of Asea and Brown Boveri. Can you imagine these two large competitors in Europe, from Sweden and Switzerland, joining together and becoming one company? They didn't even like each other. In addition to this, consider the many differences there are between Sweden and Switzerland. Percy made the merger work because he was positive, he had a vision, and he encouraged his management team to be the same way. All were encouraged to make decisions fast to take care of the good employees and to not lose market share.

Percy Barnevik was voted the top executive of the year in Europe four years in a row. Percy and ABB are excellent case studies that are being used at many graduate business schools all over the world, and they should be. There are people and there are priorities and actions that go together for success in business and in life. Percy has done this. For me, I am grateful that I have known and worked with Percy and I consider him my friend.

*Brighten someone's life today. The brightness will grow
and spread in wonderful and mysterious ways.*

Chapter Eleven – Priority Number Four
Grace

I think the first three priorities, love, family and joy, have been easy to understand and accept because we can identify with them and basically just say yes, these are right or about right. The next one is grace. What do we have to say about grace? Do we understand it and what it means? Do we understand how it might help us to be successful in business and in life? It is maybe the most difficult to understand, but maybe the easiest to obtain. Do you think obtaining and understanding grace can be possible — possible for you, your family, friends and business associates?

The Grace of God is a gift and one that we can't do anything to influence. It is a gift freely given by God. In our life and in our business dealings there is also grace that we receive and give. This is the grace that we will be discussing in this chapter, but don't ever forget about God's Grace. It is the ultimate gift!

When I think about grace, I can't help but think of Jesus looking at Peter after Peter denied him three times before the rooster crowed. Let me include the passage from Luke 22:56 - 63 for you to read:

> When one of the servant women saw him sitting there at the fire, she looked straight at him and said, "This man too was with Jesus!"

> But Peter denied it, "Woman, I don't even know him!"
> After a little while a man noticed Peter and said, "You are one of them, too!"
> But Peter answered, "Man, I am not!"
> And about an hour later another man insisted strongly, "There isn't any doubt that this man was with Jesus, because he also is a Galilean!"
> But Peter answered, "Man I don't know what you are talking about!"
> At once, while he was still speaking, a rooster crowed. The Lord turned around and looked straight at Peter, and Peter remembered that the Lord had said to him, "Before the rooster crows tonight, you will say three times that you do not know me." Peter went out and wept bitterly.

Can you imagine that look from Jesus as he looked straight at Peter? I can picture it clearly, can't you? Think about the feeling that Peter had. But in the look I see Grace. I don't see the Lord being angry or showing a look of disappointment; I see loving, caring forgiveness and understanding. I see Grace! It is a wonderful, sensitive, expressive look that Peter surely would never forget. But then, how could you ever forget the Lord looking directly at you? And you know He does look at you.

In our life we see Grace and we see grace in many ways and we are also in a position to share our grace with others. Grace could be described as love, kindness, mercy, peace, favor, understanding and other words. These words mean that because of grace the situation is better or the individual is happier or more content than before grace was shared with the one needing it. You know what this means. You see it so often with people who are really good at sharing their grace. They make people have a different outlook on life. What a wonderful gift and it seems to be so natural for these people. I suppose the sharing of grace should be a natural thing to do.

A few months ago I was flying from Chicago to Dallas and Lou Holtz was on the same flight. I said hello to him, introduced myself and said that we could use his help in Dallas. It was at the time when Jerry Jones was looking for a new coach for the Dallas Cowboys and I was guessing that Lou might be going there for an interview. He said he had more on his plate than he could presently handle and with his past year's record at South Carolina, I guess I understood. Since the Cowboys have their summer camp in Wichita Falls, I told Lou that if he ever came to Wichita Falls, I would like to help him in any way I could. He said in a very sincere way, "Well, thanks, John. I appreciate that."

Several weeks later I received a nice letter from him saying he enjoyed meeting me on the plane and appreciated my hospitality offer for Wichita Falls. He also said he was going to Dallas for a speaking engagement, not to interview with the Cowboys.

What had Lou done here? I think he shared some of his grace with me and I have told many people about how considerate he was and that he took the time to even send a personal letter after such a brief meeting. This was one of those little considerate acts of kindness that mean so much to people. It is a form of grace, I believe. Why not do these little acts of kindness that make people feel better and that add so much to their lives? Lou Holtz shared his grace and he surely reminded me that I should also be doing it. Can this example be a reminder that grace involves a sort of chain reaction? You do something kind for someone who doesn't expect it and they very well will do it for someone else. It grows and grows in the right way. Grace has a way of doing that.

I recently heard Gene Stallings sharing his grace with us during a Christian presentation. He was very impressive as he shared with the audience some highlights of his life which, by the way, were mostly not about playing or coaching football. He said what was most important to him in life was to see his children at ages 29 to 30 living good Christian lives with Christian family values. This comment made quite an impression on me, probably because Gretchen and I are also blessed this way.

Gene also said that in his travels he has the opportunity to talk to many people of all ages and has asked them what they would do differently in their lives if they could do them over. He mentioned reading about a similar question being asked to a number of people in their nineties. There was a common thread in most all of their answers, he said, and it was that they probably should have taken more risks in life. They meant nothing dangerous, but taking a more active part in the church, community and children's activities. They also would spend more time with their children. No one mentioned working harder or spending more time at work; all comments had to do with what was most important to them. They focused on their real priorities and right actions. So it is priorities and actions for success in business and in life that were most important to these seniors.

Gene shared his grace with us that afternoon, as I'm sure he has shared it with many, many others in his very successful career and personal life. You can also be sure there were many friends of Gene who appreciated receiving his grace as well.

It is very interesting to watch how all the superstars in professional athletics handle their fame, money and attention. It is difficult for them to lead a normal life especially when many of them have suddenly gone from being very, very poor to being multi-millionaires. How can they have grace? A number of them do, and these are the ones who do good works quietly. They want to give back in a Christian way and that is a way where you don't do good to get more attention. We usually don't see their grace, but we do see them as strong role models for our young people and young and upcoming athletes. Isn't this a form of grace for them? Yes, I think so, and it is also a gift that they should be sharing. To those to whom much is given, much is asked. This is also true for great athletes, but they need to be reminded by their coaches, their parents, their fans, their teammates, their real friends and the owners of their ball clubs. Let their grace grow and show in the right way!

It is just past July 4th weekend and I'm writing the chapter on grace. So what song is in my mind? Right, "America the Beautiful": "God shed His grace on thee." God did shed his grace on America. You know he did! Since God shed his grace on America, why can't we say prayers at school functions? It just seems so wrong to have a few individuals tell us we can't thank God for the many blessings he has given us and to ask for his help to protect and guide our young ones. Please think about this and use your grace and creative abilities to help correct this situation.

Thinking about America and God's grace, I wonder about how we are viewed by our neighbors outside the United States. Are we viewed as the ugly Americans when we travel to Europe or other parts of the world or do we leave a good impression? We really should think about this question.

We should travel with grace. I am reminded of some advice Gretchen and I received from a travel agent before we took our first cruise. He said, "Almost always when you are traveling, something will go wrong or at least not as you expected." His advice was to look at what is happening as being "amusing." If you stop, analyze this situation, and then say to each other, this is really amusing, it is amazing how differently you start feeling and how much easier and more enjoyable it is to communicate with others. You are now in a frame of mind in which you can share your grace and show how much character you really have. You know it is much easier to have a good time when you are laughing about a situation than when you are just plain angry. It doesn't hurt to occasionally laugh at yourself. We often take ourselves too seriously, especially when traveling. Plan to have a good time, plan to enjoy everything, even the problems when they can be amusing, and plan to share your grace with others.

Grace has to do with making others feel respected and loved. This is of course important, but we also need to remember that there are times when it is not okay to accept what is happening to make someone "feel good." How often do we say, "It is not okay?"

Several years ago we were visiting our company in Italy and I was meeting with Roberto Moroni, the president of ABB Sace. Roberto is a wonderful gentleman, a strong business leader, and one who expects things to be done correctly. One day a driver was to pick Gretchen up at the hotel at 1:00 and bring her to join us for lunch. The driver didn't get to the hotel until 1:30 and I said to Roberto that it was okay. He said in a forceful way and with a typical Italian gesture, " It is not okay!" He meant it; it was not okay.

I am reminded of this incident very often and we continue to use these words, "It is not okay" — with the same kind of expression and seriousness that Roberto used in Bergamo, Italy. As an example, to me it is not okay for our political leaders to have double standards concerning character and honesty. It simply is not okay! Being in a position of leadership in business or in life or in politics means accepting certain other responsibilities, responsibilities that include setting a good example for our associates and especially for the young ones who will be the leaders of the future. Remember that we all have the responsibility of saying "It is not okay" when it is not okay, and we should accept it.

We have the responsibility to say this with our children and we have this responsibility also in our business life. Most parents accept this responsibility and do a good job of providing the right balance of discipline and freedom. This is also true for business leaders. There should be the structure (discipline) and still the freedom for creative thinking and actions that motivate and reward employees and that satisfy customers.

Many mothers seem to have grace and are very unselfish about sharing their grace. My mother is so full of grace and love and kindness. She has done so much for our family and so many other people in sharing her grace. She has such a wonderful way of communicating her feelings and she did this with my sister and me when we were growing up. Many times we even wished she would spank us instead of using reason and logic. I remember one time before college when I came home from a fraternity rush party where I perhaps did too much partying and Mom knew it. She handled this incident in such a nice way by having a discussion with me on moderation. Her message stayed with me and I even used her advice about moderation in partying during a sales meeting in Sweden. I do have to admit that Mother had more of an effect on me than I had on our sales people. The reason for sharing this personal experience with you is to encourage you to think back on similar experiences that you have had.

It is great to see grace pass from mother to daughter in a positive way. We are again blessed in our family that this has happened from my wife to our daughter. You know, unfortunately, it can happen the other way. Just this weekend the subject of divorce came up for some reason and our son-in-law said he didn't even know what divorce was until one of his best friend's parents were divorced when he was a teenager. He added that his children also didn't know what divorce was until this same friend was himself divorced two years ago. Isn't this ironic that our son-in law and our grandchildren first learned about divorce from the same family? Is it ironic or is it a case of not accepting certain responsibilities and someone not saying "It is not okay" at the right times? Perhaps this one family example is a simplification of a complex subject, but it is worth considering what happened.

Some people have a natural grace that just shows through and you probably don't recognize it as grace, but you know something is there. You meet someone and have even a brief conversation, but during this conversation the person is one hundred percent with you, interested in you, and intent on getting to know more about you. The person's not looking around the room, but is looking at you with full attention. When the person leaves, he or she knows who you are, what you do, what interests you have, and what family you have and probably what church you go to. What do you know about him or her? Do you do the same kind of sharing and did you show the same kind of real interest? This is an opportunity and when it is over, shouldn't we ask, "Did I take advantage of this opportunity to meet this person and I mean really meet him/her or did I just say 'Nice to meet you'?"

I have trouble remembering names when I first meet someone and this is a very bad characteristic. I don't like it, but it is true.

I am trying to do better, and recognizing I have this weakness, I am trying to focus my full attention on the person I am meeting or talking with. You may do this already and are good with names, but if you feel you need some improvement you might want to think about the people you know who are good with sharing grace and try to be more like them in this respect.

For me a good example of this is John Muir, who was the senior minister at The First Christian Church in Wichita Falls. John had grace and he shared it abundantly. He also shouldered the burden of all the problems of the entire congregation. This is a tremendous responsibility to share in this way and accept all the personal concerns of so many people. John has a great sense of humor, which I'm sure helps a great deal.

One time he and I were out in the middle of a lake and the motor died and we couldn't get it started and we couldn't get any help. So we got into the water and swam the boat back into shore, which was a fairly long way. I said to him that I didn't think this should happen to me, being with my minister. I would have expected some special help. He quickly answered, "You just don't know what would have happened if I hadn't been there." Maybe I did get the special help, but if not, I did get some good quality time with a man of grace who was unselfish in all ways.

Several times during difficult budget discussions at the church, John suggested that we not increase his salary and give that amount to the assistant ministers or to the staff. He really meant it; it was not just words. He is that kind of person - full of grace. I am very appreciative of John and the opportunity I have had to spend time with him, even in the middle of the lake. You have friends like this too, don't you? Learn from what they do!

Taking the opportunity to share grace with others will return grace to you in many ways. It is like storing up for the future. Acting kindly, giving grace freely, giving when asked are all ways to become more successful in business and in life. In Matthew 5:42, Jesus says, "When someone asks you for something, give it to him; when someone wants to borrow something, lend it to him." This spring Gretchen and I were sitting at an outside café in Seville, Spain, and a man with one leg stopped at our table and asked for money. I said no, but as he walked away, I thought to myself, why did I say no? I really did think about Jesus saying "when someone asks you for something, give it to him." I ran after him and gave him a few dollars. It wasn't much, but I surely felt much better by doing at least something for this man.

More about grace:

> The Word became a human being and, full of grace and truth, lived among us. We saw his glory, the glory which he received as the Father's only Son. (John 1:14)

> Out of the fullness of his grace he has blessed us all, giving us one blessing after another. (John 1:16)

> God gave the Law through Moses, but grace and truth came through Jesus Christ. (John 1:17)

> "No! We believe and are saved by the grace of the Lord Jesus, just as they are." (Acts 15:11)

> It is the same way now: there is a small number left of those whom God has chosen because of his grace. His choice is based on his grace, not on what they have done. For if God's choice were based on what

people do, then his grace would not be real grace. (Romans 11:5-6)

But by the free gift of God's grace all are put right with him through Christ Jesus, who sets them free. (Romans 3:24)

But by God's grace I am what I am, and the grace that he gave me was not without effect. On the contrary, I have worked harder than any of the other apostles, although it was not really my own doing, but God's grace working with me. (1 Corinthians 15:10)

All this is for your sake; and as God's grace reaches more and more people, they will offer to the glory of God more prayers of thanksgiving. (2 Corinthians 4:15)

In our work together with God, then, we beg you who have received God's grace not to let it be wasted. (2 Corinthians 6:1)

But his answer was: "My grace is all you need, for my power is greatest when you are weak." I am most happy, then to be proud of my weaknesses, in order to feel the protection of Christ's power over me. (2 Corinthians 12:9)

Let us praise God for his glorious grace, for the free gift he gave us in his dear Son! For by the blood of Christ we are set free, that is, our sins are forgiven. How great is the grace of God, which he gave to us in such large measure! (Ephesians 1:6 - 8)

God's grace is the ultimate gift and we know this. Sharing our grace and receiving grace from others to help us become more successful in business and in life will be discussed in the next chapter.

What could be more satisfying and rewarding than helping to bring joy into someone's life? Reward yourself and someone else in this way today.

Chapter Twelve – Action Number Seven
Share the Grace

This is one of those very interesting actions that maybe we take for granted and we assume that we are actually sharing grace in business and in life. Probably we think we share grace more so in our personal life than in business life. How important is sharing your grace? How important is sharing your grace with your family, with your associates and with your friends? Why would you have grace if it wasn't to be shared? That is what grace is all about. Grace is not grace if it is not shared!

In the previous chapter we described grace as love, kindness, mercy, peace, favor, understanding. It is these words and others, all used together, that simply mean that because of grace the situation is better, or the individual is happier and more content than before grace was shared with the one needing it. It is much like starting with the golden rule and going from there, because grace is much more than just doing unto others as you would have them do unto you. It is way more than a fifty/fifty kind of a deal. Grace doesn't know the limitations that we impose on ourselves when we talk about a two-way street or think "what about me?"

We talked about a number of people in the last chapter who have grace and share it. You also know many people and surely there are those in your family who always seem to be doing the right things within the family and for others. They have grace and they share it. Why not think about these people and spend a few minutes just remembering and reflecting on those special things that they do to share their grace. It will help if you take a blank piece of paper or use the form included at the end of this chapter to write down the person's name and then list things that the person has done in an unselfish way to share grace with others. It might be easier if you start with things that have happened more recently and then go on back and add things that you remember about these people and the things that most impressed you. Some of these can be small acts of kindness because they always mean so much and somehow they always seem to come at the right time, the right time being the time when we need them the most — the time when there is only one set of footprints in the sand!

A gracious act might also be just being there when someone needs you. Remember if there is a question of doing something or not, just do it. If there is a question of sharing your grace with someone, just do it because no doubt they need it. Why else you would you be thinking about it in the first place if there wasn't a need?

There is a direct relationship between truth and grace. To have grace that can and will be shared, it is necessary to know and believe in the truth. In our personal lives this means believing that Jesus Christ is the Savior and our Lord. The only way to salvation is through Him and only Him. This is the truth, and grace comes from accepting and believing this completely.

We were listening to a tape of a sermon by the Reverend Rob Bugh of the Wheaton Bible Church in Wheaton, Illinois, and his message was about truth and grace. Interestingly he says that many people are committed to the truth, but are missing something. These are people who have all kinds of good plans for their business and their life, but don't have plans to know God. He suggests that there should be three elements to this important process. They are to first have a place to meet with God, then to have a regular time for this meeting and finally to have a process. Process here would mean asking God for his help. In this process we should be seeking the truth, truth in terms of integrity. We want to be truth seekers and truth makers. How important it is to be true to God and true to ourselves. Otherwise we would just be living a lie. We want to show and tell the truth in business and in our personal lives.

Let's now talk about truth and grace in business. To me these attributes bring success in business. Grace means winning and that is okay. Don't you think God wants you to be successful, wants you to win? Of course He does, because winners are in such a great position to contribute and to share their grace and gifts with others. Winners win and, unfortunately, losers lose. Let's plan to win! Remember, to those that much is given, much is asked. We want to be asked, don't we?

We would like to share some thoughts about winning in business, but first a comment about truth in business and the importance of trusting your associates. I have found that to have a successful business relationship there needs to be competence and trust. You must be able to believe what your business associates are telling you. It is okay not to have all the answers, but it is not okay to make them up or to give incorrect information. There have been a few in our company whom you just couldn't believe all the time and this is a very sad situation because falseness stifles progress. If you don't have the facts or the ones you have might not be correct, then you can't possibly be in a position to make good decisions. So it is critical that your associates must be ones that you trust and ones that you know will always be truthful. If you have some who are not, then it is your responsibility to get them to change or you must change them. You cannot live with either incompetence or those that you cannot trust.

Obviously it is best to keep existing employees. The best way is to coach them in the ways of truth, and perhaps with your grace coaching will work. This can be difficult but if it works the results will surely be worth the effort. God can help you in this situation if your problem associate will be receptive. If not, and after a reasonable time of trying, maybe this person would be happier and more successful working for some other company where truth and trust are not so important. Hopefully that place will be with your competitor.

This might be the right time to look at yourself in the mirror and ask if you sometimes undervalue truth. At certain times have you perhaps answered too quickly without really being completely sure about the answer? Do you think you can be depended upon to be always truthful when equipped with the correct facts or to say: "Let me check it out because I would rather be sure than give you incorrect information?"

Sometimes it is a matter of just answering the question or commenting on something too fast, sometimes even while the one asking the question is still talking. We had an outside salesman who was very smart and aggressive but customers didn't seem to like him very much. You know this is not a good situation, having a salesman to whom customers don't want to give their business. I watched this salesman in action with three different customers and it was very clear that he didn't listen to what they were saying. He was a very good talker, but a very bad listener, and unfortunately he was talking a lot more than he was listening. He didn't realize this was happening because I think his mind was running faster than his other senses. He was technically very competent and knew the products very well, but his mouth working harder than his ears resulted in customers not wanting to do business with him. He was lacking grace and it showed.

Jim Lundy, president of Performance Systems Inc. stresses in his seminars the importance of listening in business and in personal life. He has developed the nine levels of listening.

Nine Levels of Listening

#1. Not there physically. (You didn't attend or show up.)

#2. There physically, but not mentally. (Not paying attention at all.)

#3. Hearing, but doing something else at the same time. (Such as watching elsewhere, reading, or thinking about a different matter.)

#4. Interrupting soon and frequently.

#5. Interrupting later and less often.

#6. Allowing to finish, but meanwhile intensely thinking of a counter or a response.

#7. Allowing to finish while earnestly trying to understand what is being said, but then replying immediately.

#8. Allowing to finish, pausing, thoughtfully considering what has been said, and then replying.

#9. Allowing to finish, pausing, summarizing what you think you heard, and only then replying.

We want to be level eight or nine listeners! This should be a goal for all of us.

Together with being truthful and trustworthy, you must also be dependable. Can others depend on you to do what you say you will do? Do your associates do what they say they will do? Is your business or organization one that has standards so that all employees always or almost always do what is expected of them or what they said they would do? You know there are both kinds of companies, organizations or departments where dependability can be counted on and others where it is okay to take action only when it is convenient. You probably have seen both and there is no question about which is the most productive and the most successful. I would suggest that you think about dependability here. How many of your associates do you feel you have to follow up with when they are asked to do something? How many do you know for sure will do whatever it is and you don't have to worry about it? Where do you fit into this analysis? Should you be doing something about your dependability? Should you monitor your own actions or those of others by letting them know "It is not okay" to not meet deadlines or commitments.

Where does being a considerate person fit into a successful business? What do you think? How many of the top managers in your company are what you would call a considerate person? Do you have a considerate company? Are you considerate of your customers, your suppliers?

A number of years ago there was an article in the *Harvard Business Review* about monkeys in business. It seems that everyone has a few monkeys that they carry around on their shoulders and no one really likes to have these monkeys just hanging around. So what do they do? They unload their monkeys on others and let them have the burden of caring for these extra monkeys. An example of this problem would be a sales correspondent who comes into the sales manager's office telling him about this customer who is so upset because his shipment is going to be late. The monkey is the upset customer and he is on the shoulder of the sales correspondent. So the manager has two basic choices: he can say, "Don't worry about it, I'll call the customer and explain to him why his order is being delayed," or he can say to the sales correspondent, "What do you think you should do to satisfy this customer?" Here, the monkey is waiting to either jump over to the sales manager or to stay where he is. After the correspondent calls the customer, the monkey will just go away. This is like a game of monkey, monkey, who's got the monkey. You want to take care of only your own monkeys, not others' and not give yours to your associates. This is one way of measuring how considerate you are and how considerate the others are that you deal with. Do you take care of your own monkeys? Do you help others deal with their own monkeys?

Another way to determine if consideration is a hallmark of a company is to think about how questions are asked and how people are asked to do their jobs. Is it in a friendly, considerate way with good verbal communications or is it by e-mail as an order rather than a request? Are there open regular communications among your associates, or do people communicate only when it is absolutely necessary. As an example, I know one manager whom everyone avoids as much as possible because any communication gets analyzed and torn apart in a critical and negative way. There is rarely anything positive or nice that is said. This is an extreme case probably, but the idea is that there are those with whom you like to share information and everyone gains, and others whom you contact only when necessary — not a very good situation, but one that we all have to be aware of.

Are you one of those that others freely share information with? Do others look forward to receiving your ideas and comments?

I have said many times, "Don't ask the question if you are not prepared for the answer." If you ask your boss what he thinks you should do and he answers, you better be prepared to do what he says. I think it is also important to add that you shouldn't answer the question if the person asking the question is not prepared for the answer. This is being considerate; it is sharing your grace.

Knowledge is: Don't ask the question if you're not prepared for the answer.

Grace is: Don't answer the question if the person asking the question is not prepared for the answer.

We have discussed how people share grace by being truthful, trustful, dependable and considerate. These are very basic ingredients in a well-performing organization that can be successful. If you don't have these kinds of people or this kind of organization, then it will be very difficult to have a winning business or organization. You need to work to develop these attributes or you need to take a more active role in sharing your grace so it makes a difference.

There has to be a core of associates who are truthful, can be trusted, are dependable and are considerate to build a winning organization or to rebuild an existing one. It can be done if this inner team is willing to share their grace. If this core group is in place, they can benefit from additional ideas on building a winning business.

- The people are most important and are number one, not only the person at the top but the other associates as well. Quality managers attract quality people. If your company has compromised in some positions or has the wrong people in place, the organizational problems will grow because the wrong manager will attract the wrong people. Quality people really do attract quality people and vice versa. Whom do you want to work for and whom do you want working for you? You want quality people who share their grace with you and others!

- A winning organization has to be customer focused. A really customer- focused organization does more than have "cute" posters on the walls. In such an organization there are more discussions about customers than about local football games or the weather. Customer service is the most important agenda item in every important company meeting. In the eyes of our customers, what are we doing well and what should we be doing better? These should be questions we ask our customers and ourselves regularly.

- Now with good customer-focused employees and good customers wouldn't it make good sense to get them together often? Why not have a customer-of-the-month celebration to let that company's people know how important they are to your company. Wouldn't this be a good time for your management team to meet their management team to discuss how each can help the other to become more successful? Do you have a top-level manager assigned to each of your top accounts? Who is really responsible for each account? Is there someone involved at the management level? Your employees would like to know more about customers, including where and how they use your products. These get-togethers will be good for the morale of your people.

- Know that customers care with whom they do business. They want to do business with people they like, trust and want to associate with. A winning company recognizes this and asks questions like the following:

  > If you were the customer, would you want to buy from our company?

  > If you were the customer, would you want to buy from our sales people? Would you send our sales person to call on a good friend of yours?

  > Do we deserve this customer's business? What should we do to really earn their business in the future?

  > Are we paying attention to the basics? Do we know what the customer wants today and will want in the future?

  > Why did we win or lose each significant order? We should know the reasons for each - winning and losing.

Share the grace you have in your personal life and share it in business. Encourage others to do the same. It will grow and all will win with this sharing.

Action Number Seven

Priorities & Actions
People Who Have Shared Grace with Others

How They Shared Grace with Others

Name

Empathy is easy for those who care, are thoughtful and sensitive to the feelings and needs of others. Don't make it difficult!

Chapter Thirteen – Priority Number Five
Forgiveness

Priority number five is forgiveness. This is the last of the five priorities that have been given to us. They can be used along with the ten actions to lead and direct us to a better, more successful life. Remember the first priority was love, then family. These very important first two priorities were followed by joy and grace, and now we have forgiveness.

This chapter will deal with asking for forgiveness and forgiving others. Probably both very often go together. Isn't it often the case that neither person is completely right or completely wrong? A simple, even innocent misunderstanding of what someone said or meant may have started the problem. Maybe someone was having a bad day or was involved in a stressful situation and inadvertently said the wrong thing. These things unfortunately do happen, so it is important to be sensitive to circumstances that might affect behavior in negative ways.

God through His son Jesus Christ has forgiven all of us for all our sins. What can be more important than this? Receiving forgiveness from God is truly an unbelievable and undeserved gift. We know that God forgives our past sins, so we can focus on forgiving others and asking for forgiveness for those who we have hurt.

I would like to share a few passages from Matthew to help us better understand what we are trying to accomplish in this chapter:

> You have heard that it was said, 'An eye for an eye, and a tooth for a tooth.' But now I tell you; do not take revenge on someone who wrongs you. If anyone slaps you on the right cheek, let him slap your left cheek too. And if someone takes you to court to sue you for your shirt, let him have your coat as well. And if one of the occupation troops forces you to carry his pack one mile, carry it two miles. When someone asks you for something, give it to him; when someone wants to borrow something, lend it to him.
> Matthew 5:38 - 42

How many situations or similar situations have you experienced that would fit into the above passage? You can relate these expressions to your everyday life. A slap on the right cheek might be a jealous comment, a mean answer, or gossip. Carrying a pack one mile might be what you would do when someone at work who is not doing his or her share expects you to do the job — yet still wants to receive all the credit. Why not do even more than expected? When someone asks you for something, it might be your gifts or talents that are needed. Maybe the favor won't be returned. This is okay, isn't it? Someone taking you to court to sue for your shirt might be compared to an unhappy, unreasonable customer who is demanding action from your company. You know, that customer might be asking for "bread," so why not give "cake"? All these things can be experienced many times in many different ways. How we respond and handle problems or challenges is what really counts and shows the kind of person we are or want to be. It is a question of character, understanding, patience - and yes, of course, grace. Maybe we are in a different frame of mind now so that we can look back at these situations in a more positive and caring way. We will discuss doing this a little later.

> Do not judge others, so that God will not judge you, for God will judge you in the same way you judge others, and he will apply to you the same rules you apply to others. Why, then, do you look at the speck in your brother's eye and pay no attention to the log in your own eye? How dare you say to your brother, 'please, let me take that speck out of your eye,' when you have a log in your own eye? You hypocrite! First take the log out of your own eye, and then you will be able to see clearly to take the speck out of your brother's eye. Matthew 7:1 - 5

Haven't we many times seen people who are way off base in their criticisms of others? These critics do the same things or maybe even worse than what they accuse others of, and it seems to be okay for them, but not okay for their friends or associates. Is this a log in their eye? Are they being critical about the speck in others? Yes, that's often true. What I believe this scripture means, however is that we need to take a few steps back and reflect on what we have been doing and what we plan to do now. We need to look into the "honesty" mirror to see if we have a log in our own eye. To forgive and ask for forgiveness in the right way might very well mean doing something differently in the future. It might mean we have to make some changes. Let's be prepared to think about changing ourselves when we analyze how we are going to ask for forgiveness and how we are going to forgive someone who maybe doesn't know he or she needs to be forgiven. These persons might not know they did anything wrong or said something that upset or offended you.

As we begin to explore this issue we need to think about our pride and our ego. How important are our pride and our ego? Does pride really matter so much? What is a bruised ego or a hurting pride and who can see it? In God's list of priorities that we are discussing, it surely isn't in the top five and I doubt very much if it would be in the top one hundred or even top thousand. Our pride and our ego in fact might very well be the Evil One's way of keeping us distracted from the really important priorities. They probably are in Satan's top five. So we need to swallow our pride and admit that maybe in some of these situations we were wrong. At least in the eyes of the other person we were wrong. So what? Again, how important can this be?

Let's look again at a family we know in which the daughter does not allow her mother or father to visit her family or to have any contact with their grandchildren. This means that these darling little children are growing up in the same city as their grandparents and can't see them, don't know them, and can't experience their love and share their gifts. This situation isn't right. Something went wrong. What was it? Who did the first wrong thing? Somebody made a mistake or a group of mistakes, but right now the situation is a stalemate with no progress being made and precious time is flying by.

What would you like to see happen? Someone has to take the lead, swallow some pride, fight off the Evil One and do some real soul searching. The real soul searching is to really look at what might have happened. Could it be that the grandparents tried to interfere with the way the daughter and son-in-law were trying to raise the kids? Maybe so. Or could it be that they were too possessive or too lenient or too ... I don't know. But they should be able to think about when the problem started and what the events were that led up to this situation. Then they should go to this young family and ask for forgiveness for doing this or that and let them know they want to be the kind of grandparents that this family wants them to be. They can change and are prepared to do so, even if the problem is the daughter. It would be worth it!

That is grace and it is grace, love, family, joy and forgiveness that are needed to get this family back together again. It is all the five priorities, and using all of them probably will be necessary. But don't you think the result will be worth it? What could there be that would have a higher priority in their lives right now?

There has to be a very strong desire and motivation on the part of either the parents or the children to make reconciliation happen. Someone has to take the first step. The example here shows the grandparents being the catalyst for change, but it could be their children doing the same thing. It is the results that count, not the means.

Let's ask for some additional help and direction.

> When you are praying, do not heap up empty phrases as the Gentiles do; for they think that they will be heard because of their many words. Do not be like them, for your Father knows what you need before you ask him.
>
> Pray then in this way:
>
> Our Father in heaven,
> hallowed be your name,
> Your kingdom come.
> Your will be done,
> on earth as it is in heaven.
> Give us this day our daily
> bread.
> And forgive us our debts,
> as we also have forgiven
> our debtors.

> And do not bring us to the time
> of trial, but rescue us from the evil one.
>
> For if you forgive others their trespasses, your heavenly Father will also forgive you, but if you do not forgive others, neither will your Father forgive your trespasses. Matthew 6: 7 - 15

There are many Bible study courses where the Lord's Prayer is studied in great depth and detail to understand thoroughly what it says. I think every time I read the Lord's Prayer, it takes on a deeper meaning. Somehow when I read the Lord's Prayer I think more about the real meaning of each phrase. I discover more that is important and real for me. Today with His priority number five, look again at what Jesus is saying about forgiveness. Forgive us the wrongs (or sins or trespasses) we have done as we forgive the wrongs (or sins or trespasses) that others have done to us. This means we must forgive others if we are to be forgiven. This is what Jesus is saying in verses 14 and 15: "If you forgive others the wrongs they have done to you, your Father in heaven will also forgive you. But if you do not forgive others, then your Father will not forgive the wrongs you have done."

I repeated these two verses for a reason. I wanted to write them again and I wanted you to read them again because they are a must, not a maybe or something that would be nice to do, but a must! And the words all make such sound and logical sense. Can you do anything but believe them?

At times, though, this scripture can be difficult to understand and accept. The problem that sometimes arises concerning this important scripture comes when one tries to take the statement in a literal way. It appears to place a limit on God's forgiveness by requiring man to forgive before God will forgive him. The Bible makes it clear that God's forgiveness is an act of "grace," which is a free and unmerited gift of God's love. Yet, rightly understood, there is no contradiction. Forgiveness is a gift of God's grace when one is more concerned about the person than what that person has done.

An example is the story of the prodigal son. The father, representing God, is able to disregard the irresponsible actions of the son through grace and celebrate instead the joyful reconciliation.

What Jesus is saying here is that unless one has the experience of forgiving others he will not have the state of mind that is receptive to God's forgiveness.

This is pretty complex, but I would think we understand the importance of forgiveness. So what do we do about it? My recommendation is that we do the following. Let's start another list and begin writing down the names of all the people who over the years we have hurt. Whom do you wish you would have said you were sorry to? From little incidents to big ones try to make a complete list. You want to take action on all of these and you want to end up with a clean sheet of paper on your list of "people from whom I want to ask for forgiveness."

Remember you were asked to start a list during the first chapter for all those people you wanted to thank, even the ones who aren't with us any more. This is the same kind of list that will include all those people whom you want to tell you are sorry and you want their forgiveness. This list should, like the thank you list, also include those who are not with us anymore. They will know how you feel!

I think of Gretchen's father who lived to be 95 and was a wonderful caring grandfather. Our children loved to visit him and to listen to his stories. Shortly before he died he told us he was sorry about scolding Chuck one time in York, Pennsylvania, many, many years ago. We didn't even know what he was talking about, but it was important to him. Apparently he scolded our oldest son one day and he felt bad because he felt he was interfering with our discipline and our responsibilities as parents. It was a very little thing and didn't even make an impression on either of us, but it did on him. Do you have some things that you want to say something about before you are 95?

I'll bet most of the items on the list will be things that are pretty insignificant and probably not even known by the other person, or if known, most likely forgotten. What Gretchen's father was talking about was insignificant and forgotten by us, but not by him. This guilt should have been crossed off his list and erased from his mind years before. We can unburden our conscience now.

I really think it is the little things we have done to others that we often feel bad about. Don't you suppose the same is the case with them and what they have done to you or said to you? Why don't you also make a list that includes all those who you think could possibly feel this way? Who are the ones who need relationship building or mending? These would be ones who might feel bad about something they did or said.

Maybe there are some situations that are fairly serious and obvious. Whatever happened is keeping you apart or is hurting your friendship or marriage or family. You know what it is. Think about what this person did and try to put it in the right perspective.

Recently I heard about a family discussing what they should do about a son who made a few mistakes, one of which was fairly serious. One family member tried to create the right frame of mind by telling about all the very good things the son did throughout his life and stressing that he really had made just a few unfortunate poor decisions. This family member still gave him an A+. With all the opportunities to do good or bad things and with the many temptations we are all facing from the Evil One, the son with the problems still had a grade average of about 98%. To the family this should be an A+. Can't you forgive an A+ student or friend or family member who perhaps receives one low grade (bad decision)? I think Jesus would and I believe he would expect you to also.

In business the opportunity for saying the wrong thing or being misunderstood happens almost every day. It takes real empathy and wisdom to know how someone is receiving your messages. Likewise, it is easy for you to think you understood what someone was saying or asking. It is easy to be wrong.

I think particularly in communications with business associates in Europe or South America it is so easy to be misunderstood. The associate speaks excellent English, but it is not his native language. He or she might not know the meaning of all the colloquialisms we use that are common to us. The meanings are clear to us, but they might not mean the same things in Sweden or Italy.

A misunderstanding happened to me just this past year when we were discussing developing or acquiring a new product line in a group meeting in Switzerland. There were representatives from Germany, Sweden, Italy, Switzerland, Finland and the United States. The meeting ended after about two hours in a rather negative way. I knew this, but didn't know what had happened or why there seemed to be bad feelings. I didn't want ill feelings to continue so I decided to be the one to "swallow my pride" and admit that I made a mistake. I told the leader of this meeting that I was in favor of supporting his proposal and I felt there had been some misunderstandings that could be corrected. I said, "Let's start over and I will be much more supportive of your position during the next meeting." We shook hands, agreed to be friends, and proceeded to have a good meeting. I have respect for him; we like each other now and are friends. If I had not recognized the problem or had not asked him to "forgive me," the process would have stopped and I never would have gotten to know him the way I do now. That would have been my loss and the loss for our company.

What did I learn here?

- First you must carefully listen to what others are saying, especially if you don't know the person.
- Another is to appreciate that each one in the meeting has different goals and motives. These can be very different for different countries.
- The next lesson is to not accept the results of a bad meeting. Do something about it so that it can turn out in a positive and successful way.
- It's okay to say it is my fault; let's start over.
- Words have different meanings in other countries. Make sure you are talking, listening and understanding together.
- Confirm understanding by asking the same question in two or three different ways. The answers should still be the same.
- Another is to try very hard to understand what each person in the meeting wants and why.

- Add a little joy to every meeting.

Another time three of us from the United States were negotiating with two top managers from a Belgium company. Only one of them spoke good English. Early on in the meeting, Michelle, the one who spoke only a little English, gave us a company pin to wear. After about half a day of negotiating who was going to pay for the start up of this new business, we were told this small company had limited financial resources and the start up would have to be paid for by us. I thought they were exaggerating and bluffing so to make a point I offered to give the pin back to help their financial situation. Michelle felt this was a way of saying no to their offer and he stood up, shook hands and left the table. The discussions almost broke down. We had to bring him back with an apology for our being inconsiderate. I asked him to forgive us for our American brashness. This little incident became an important part of our relationship in the future. With good times we shared pins and asked for pins during difficult times.

Communications are so important! It is also important to be able to say, "I'm sorry and please forgive me for what I said or did."

Communications and understanding go together. It doesn't do any good to try to communicate without understanding. Without understanding there is no communication. Jim Lundy, author of *Lead, Follow or Get Out of the Way* has written on understanding:

ON UNDERSTANDING

Oh how wonderful life can be when we have mutual understanding.

Nearly all good things (even love) are enhanced by understanding.

Unless I listen better, I'll probably keep on misunderstanding others.

Not interrupting each other will foster improved communication.

Daring to seek confirmation will minimize assumptions and interpretations.

Emotional comments and responses should be dealt with calmly.

Remember the suggestion to use two ears and one mouth proportionately.

Senders should verify that the receivers have gotten the message.

Tell 'em what you're going to tell 'em, tell 'em, tell 'em what you told 'em.

Active listening can enhance our comprehension of each other's views.

Now that we understand each other better we can proceed to succeed.

Dedication to improved communication requires effort, but can yield great rewards.

Is the prospect of fewer misunderstanding worthy of your commitment?

No effort is more commendable than the search for understanding.

God help all of us to understand each other better and better!

Try to complete both of the lists at the end of the chapter. Have a plan to take care of all those to whom you want to say, "I'm really sorry about what I did. It was inconsiderate of me and a stupid thing to do. Can you forgive me?" With the other list you might be simply saying, "I think we had a disagreement or misunderstanding and I want to make it right. I am sorry. Can we start over?" This is where the pride or ego has to just go away, because who needs it?

What about the lists from chapter two? Do you want to go back and review these before you move on to the next chapter?

How long will it be before your forgiveness lists will have everything crossed off and erased from your mind? It will be much easier to keep a clean sheet in the future, won't it?

A customer is a customer, is a customer, is a customer!
By any other name he would still be your customer. When he asks for bread,
give him cake. Likewise, do the same for friends and family

Chapter Fourteen – Action Number Eight
Keep the Right Priorities

If you have priorities, they should truly be priorities, not just words. In *Time Out...It's Your Call* there are just five priorities. We have discussed them all. Remember they are, in order of importance, love, family, joy, grace and forgiveness.

You can list other priorities that are important to you, but how close are they really to these top five priorities? Don't you think these are enough for you to focus on now?

Back when I was the Midwest Regional Sales Manager for Cutler-Hammer I wrote a letter to myself. Although it started out "Dear John", it was not actually a "Dear John" letter. It was just a letter from John to John doing some self-analysis. I'm not kidding. I really did write myself a letter. It was never mailed because it didn't have to be. I personally delivered it to myself and then put it in my desk to save for future reference. The manager who followed me in this position found this letter a few years later and called to see what happened and if writing a letter to oneself works. I answered, "Yes, it does work," and here is an explanation of what happened.

At the time I was a heavy smoker and thought I wanted to stop, but I wasn't doing a very good job of quitting. Even with the continuing pressure from the kids and my wife, I just kept right on smoking two packs a day. Here is what I told myself:

Dear John,

It is about time for you to give some serious thought to your life because if you don't do it now, you may end up without your life. Then it will obviously be too late and no amount of sorrow or regrets will fix the situation. You know that smoking is bad for your health. You know if you continue to smoke you are going to die. You don't know when but the odds are for a much shorter life if you continue to be a heavy smoker. John, why don't you make two lists? One should be "Reasons Why I Smoke" and the other should be "Reasons Why I Should Not Smoke."

Okay, I'll do it.

Reasons Why I Smoke

#1. I enjoy the taste. Actually I enjoy only a few puffs each day.

#2. I'm afraid I'll gain a lot of weight if I stop smoking.

#3. I'll be nervous if I quit.

#4. I am stupid.

#5 I am very stupid.

Reasons Why I Should Not Smoke

#1. My health. I will live a longer more healthy life if I don't smoke.

#2. It is expensive.

#3. I have shortness of breath. I get winded playing basketball and other sports.

#4. I cough in the morning.

#5. I am always worried about running out of cigarettes and not being able to get more. I hate being so dependent on a weed.

#6. Someday, I know I will say to myself, "Why didn't you quit when you still had your health?"

#7. It isn't fair to my wife and kids. Besides the danger of second-hand smoke, it just isn't fair to leave them when you die young. That is very inconsiderate.

#8. I have bad breath and my clothes smell bad.

#9. I don't want our kids to smoke, so why not set a good example for them.

#10. More and more customers are not smoking and it is not good to smoke in their offices. The same is true about friends' homes.

#11. I burn holes in clothes and furniture.

#12. I sometimes peel the skin off my lips.

John, look at the two lists. You would have to be absolutely stupid to not see there are really no reasons to continue smoking and many reasons to quit. Don't you see that you are really not giving anything up, but are actually gaining so much? So, why not quit now?

Do it now!

Sincerely,
John Bridgman

I did quit smoking. I stopped because, when I actually analyzed my choices, I realized I just had no choice. I convinced myself and I truly believed that I would be gaining so much by stopping. I wasn't giving up anything important. Every smoker today should make similar lists. Maybe you can encourage someone you care about to do this. I stopped cold turkey without telling anyone what I was doing. This was part of the challenge: to act on a decision without making a big deal out of it. Remember, don't boast, let it happen! It was five days before anyone noticed that I had stopped smoking.

This chapter is not, however, about stopping smoking; it is about keeping the right priorities. My experience in listing the reasons for not smoking and for smoking has made me a believer in putting things in writing and making lists. That helps you think things out; it helps your subconscious work on your problems. If you have it in writing, you can easily refer to what you wrote. Don't you agree? Have you made some lists yourself? Are they working for you? Please remember to let me know.

Let's start out with a new list that may include some of your thoughts from previous chapters: Reasons Why I Should Keep the Right Priorities. Here are a few examples to consider:

Priorities

LOVE   FAMILY JOY   GRACE   FORGIVENESS

Reasons Why I Should Keep the Right Priorities

- I believe that is what God expects of me.
- I love my family and there isn't anything in good conscience I wouldn't do for them.

- I want my family to do the right things to fully enjoy each other and their life.

- I also want to do the right things and to feel satisfaction in business and in life.

- There should be more joy in the world and I can make a difference.

- It is important that God knows I love Him, have faith in Him and trust Him always.

- My spouse, my family and my associates should know that I love them. I need to tell them and I need to show them how I feel by my actions and by my priorities.

- Keeping the right priorities will help me to be successful in business and in life. This is the way to be a winner in my job.

- God has shared his Grace with my family and me. I need to share whatever gifts and grace I have with others.

- It is time to forgive and to ask for forgiveness. This is the right thing to do.

- I know I have to stay focused on these priorities because the Evil One will continually try to distract me. He works this way because he has very different priorities for me to follow.

Do you have other reasons that should be added or ones that should be changed? Please take the time to go ahead and complete your list now. What other reasons do you have for keeping the priorities?

Can you think of any reasons for not keeping the priorities? In my "Dear John" letter I listed the reasons for smoking, which I could relate to the reasons for not keeping the priorities. The decision then was easy for me and maybe this would be the same for you and your list. If you have some reasons for not keeping priorities, go ahead and start the second list. See how it compares to your first list.

The list showing reasons for keeping the priorities are general in nature. They need to be much more specific and action-oriented to be effective in our everyday life. During each one of the chapters on priorities you thought about and possibly listed specific actions you would take. Why not review these now or look back at each of these five chapters as a reminder of what was discussed. The reason is to help you add real-life actions to each of the reasons that you listed for keeping the priorities.

I believe we need a daily reminder of these five priorities, some way to wake us up each day to the need for staying focused and taking the right actions ahead of all the other little time-killers. Probably you have taken time management courses, or if not you have the common sense to know that you have a choice each day. In fact you have many choices. You have the choice of being very productive and doing high-priority things, or you have the choice of just letting things happen, doing the easy things that don't really require much thought or effort. We all have lots of those things. E-mail and Lotus Notes give us many of these kinds of time-killers and we seem to grab them up and make them grow. It's like grabbing someone else's monkeys and breeding them electronically. Monkeys are running all over the Internet and all over our business communications today.

Business time management tells us to take on the most important "A" projects or assignments and work on them first. Keep working on the "A's" for as long as they last and only move to the "B" rated ones when there are no more "A's." You probably never get to the "C's" and probably you shouldn't. If a "C" needs action or attention, it will move up to become a "B" or "A." Then you can deal with it. Don't go looking for "C's." You know monkeys carry around a lot of "C's" and leave a lot of "C" messes all over the place.

In life the five priorities are all "A's." The difference in life and in business is that you never finish with A priorities and there is never a need to move on to "B" priorities. We also have to be careful that "B" or "C" priorities do not move up and replace "A" priorities. The top five should stay on top.

There are many ways to remind ourselves to keep the right priorities. A simple yet effective way would be to have a small card that lists love, family, joy, grace and forgiveness. Put it on your mirror so that you see it each morning. Or put it on your refrigerator. A magnetic cross can hold it up.

When Peter Janson was president of ABB Inc., he used QUALITY as his password for his computer. I happen to know this because I used his computer one day in Stamford, Connecticut, and had to log on using QUALITY as the password. Every day when he turned on his computer he would think "quality." It was usually the first thing he did early each morning, and this started the day off with the thought, "What am I going to do today to promote quality within ABB?" You could use PRIORITIES as your password. Not a bad idea! Knowing that your personal password is PRIORITIES would be a great way to start each day. It surely would help to remind you that you should be keeping the right priorities at work. Maybe there should be a reminder at work and at home. Perhaps you need two computers with the same password.

Time Out ... It's Your Call

This reminds me of the story about 1,000 Marbles, author unknown.

1,000 Marbles

The older I get, the more I enjoy Saturday mornings. Perhaps it's the quiet solitude that comes with being the first to rise, or maybe it's the unbounded joy of not having to be at work. Either way, the first few hours of a Saturday morning are most enjoyable.

A few weeks ago, I was shuffling toward the basement with a steaming cup of coffee in one hand and the morning paper in the other. What began as a typical Saturday morning turned into one of those lessons that life seems to hand you from time to time. Let me tell you about it.

I turned the dial up into the phone portion of the band on my ham radio in order to listen to a Saturday morning swap net. Along the way, I came across an older sounding chap, with a tremendous signal and a golden voice. You know the kind; he sounded like he should be in the broadcasting business. He was telling whomever he was talking with something about "a thousand marbles." I was intrigued and stopped to listen to what he had to say. "Well, Tom, it sure sounds like you're busy with your job. I'm sure they pay you well but it's a shame you have to be away from home and your family so much.

"Hard to believe a young fellow should have to work sixty or seventy hours a week to make ends meet. Too bad you missed your daughter's dance recital." He continued, "Let me tell you something, Tom, something that has helped me keep a good perspective on my own priorities."

And that's when he began to explain his theory of a "thousand marbles." "You see, I sat down one day and did a little arithmetic. The average person lives about seventy-five years. I know, some live more and some live less, but on the average, folks live about seventy-five years. Now then, I multiplied 75 times 52 and I came up with 3,900, which is the number of Saturdays that the average person has in his entire lifetime.

"Now stick with me, Tom, I'm getting to the important part. It took me until I was fifty-five years old to think about all this in any detail," he went on, "and by that time I had lived through over 2,800 Saturdays. I got to thinking that if I lived to be seventy-five, I only had about a thousand of them left to enjoy.

"So, I went to a toy store and bought every single marble they had. I ended up having to visit three toy stores to round up 1,000 marbles. I took them home and put them inside a large, clear plastic container right here in the shack next to my gear. Every Saturday since then, I have taken one marble out and thrown it away.

"I found that by watching the marbles diminish, I focused more on the really important things in life. There is nothing like watching your time here on this earth run out to help get your priorities straight.

"Now let me tell you one last thing before I sign off with you and take my lovely wife out for breakfast. This morning, I took the very last marble out of the container. I figure if I make it until next Saturday then I have been given a little extra time. And the one thing we can all use is a little more time.

"It was nice to meet you, Tom, I hope you spend more time with your family, and I hope to meet you again here on the band. 75 year Old Man... this is K9NZFQ, clear and going QRT, good morning!"

You could have heard a pin drop on the band when this fellow signed off. I guess he gave us all a lot to think about. I had planned to work on the antenna that morning, and then I was going to meet up with a few hams to work on the next club newsletter. Instead, I went upstairs and woke my wife up with a kiss. "C'mon honey, I'm taking you and the kids to breakfast."

"What brought this on?" she asked with a smile. "Oh, nothing special; it's just been a long time since we spent a Saturday together with the kids. Hey, can we stop at a toy store while we're out? I need to buy some marbles."

On the average how many more Saturdays do we have left? I think we should do the same arithmetic as the man in this story did. We should put marbles into a container that would total the number of weeks remaining until we reach the age of seventy-five years. The container should be marked PRIORITIES.

Each week take one marble out of this container, think about "keeping the right priorities" and then don't throw the marble away. Put it in another container that is marked SUCCESSFUL WEEKS.

This way the PRIORITIES container will have fewer and fewer marbles in it but the SUCCESSFUL WEEKS container will have more and more in it. Moving the marbles from one container to the other is an optimistic thing to do and will be a visible reminder that keeping the right priorities is the way to a successful life.

Are you using some other way to remind you to keep the right priorities? If so, please let me know so I can share it with others.

Life is such a blessing with such opportunities to do the right things for family, friends and associates. Take advantage of each day to make good things happen.

Chapter Fifteen – Action Number Nine
Live the Right Life all the Time

After a discussion of the five priorities and the first eight actions, with the previous action being "keep the right priorities," it would seem only natural that this chapter should be "Live the right life all the time." We all seriously want to live the right life. We recognize the right thing to do, but do we really want to do it all the time? It's like quitting smoking. I'm not quite mentally ready yet, but I will be soon. Or going on a new diet. Let's start Monday. And how about New Year's resolutions? I have made so many of them and so have many of you. I know because quite often I see the same new YMCA members at the gym in early January. We are the ones who step on the scale before and after a workout, generally with a disappointed frown on our faces.

Let's just think about this for a minute. Going on a diet or getting in shape or quitting smoking are all important, but living the right life all the time is much more than a New Year's resolution list. It is much more serious and important for you if you are to become more successful in business and in life.

Living the right life has to mean so much to us. We have only one lifetime to live so we want to make sure we fully take advantage of our time in business and in our daily lives. It is up to you to decide what living the right life all the time really is and what it means to you. You can do this now. You don't have to continue with past decisions that might not be right today. If you are in a rut in business, take actions to get out of the rut and into a different environment. Or it might just be your attitude that needs adjusting, not the environment. Think about it. You have to make this decision.

Have you ever heard about the Rut-a-Rooter? Not a Roto-Rooter but a Rut-a-Rooter. You won't find it listed in the Yellow Pages. It is found in your conscious and your subconscious mind. You will use this to open up the rut and create new and exciting opportunities for you. It is there; you have it ready to work for you.

What is leading the right life for us, our family and our associates? As you read this chapter think about the five priorities and the actions that have been discussed. Are these the measures of living the right life for you? See if following these priorities and taking these actions constitute what you would consider to be a good definition of leading the right life. If not, add to these so that you can be satisfied that you know what leading the right life really is for you.

There are a number of times in our lifetimes when we are in a position to make decisions that can dramatically affect our future. You know them. Which college should I attend? What should my major be? What companies should I interview? Should I get married? Where should we live? Should I change jobs? Should I accept the promotion? Should we have children now? The list goes on and on for decisions that you have to make. These are mostly yes or no or go -no go kinds of decisions that you make during the normal course of your life.

There are a number of ways to analyze the alternatives to help you make the right decisions. I hope the priorities and actions discussed in this book will help with some of these decisions. You have read quite a lot about making lists for and against doing something. Again let me stress the benefits of putting ideas down in writing and letting your subconscious help you with the analysis. You can also use the help that is available to you in making these decisions.

I have found that it is the little decisions that seem to be harder to make than the big ones. Maybe it's because we don't make lists of pros and cons, either in writing or in our minds, for the little decisions. It could be that we might not ask for help for the little decisions. If you think you are spending too much time on these less significant decisions in business or in life, consider making lists and asking for help even for these decisions. I'll bet the answers will come much quicker and much clearer if you do. God is interested in being with you all the time. He wants to be part of all your decisions, big and small.

In conjunction with these lists, I would also suggest that you include several more thoughts. The first is, "What is the very worst thing that could happen to me with this decision?" Even with an extremely active imagination, you will probably find the worst scenario isn't really too bad. The next question to ask is, "What can I do if the decision is wrong and it really doesn't work out?" Again the answers are still pretty good. You will have gained additional experience, made some new friends, added to your resume and probably built some character.

At one time we moved about every four to five years with our three children. We lived in Boston; York, Pennsylvania; Allentown, Pennsylvania; Birmingham, Michigan; and Wichita Falls, Texas. We loved all these locations and had good friends in all of them. Each time we moved I would tell the kids several important things:

> • You are the ones who are winning because you have these good friends here, but think about all the new ones you'll make where we are moving. It is your friends here who should be sad because they are losing you but don't have new friends to take your place.
>
> • You will have the experience of living in different cities and different parts of the country. This is fun and exciting.
>
> • A family becomes much closer when you move to a new location.
>
> • Relocating builds character.

After we moved from Michigan to Wichita Falls, Texas, our daughter Julie told me that she agreed with all of these benefits, but did not think we needed to build any more character by moving. "Let's not move again, Dad. You've built enough character in us in this way." Well, we didn't. The decision even meant I had to commute to New York for over two years, but we had found our home. It was time for us to follow the right priorities. It was time to have a "home" base.

These are digital decisions just requiring yes or no. There are also what I call analog decisions. These are the kinds of decisions that are based on how important something is to you. Or how serious you are about it or how committed you are. Are you willing to pay the price for the result you want? A few examples include the following:

> • I really do want to become president of the company.

- My family means everything to me. I don't want anything to interfere with my time with them.

- My daughter has the ability to be an Olympic gymnast. I am going to do whatever I can to make this happen.

- Our family is going to give back to the community by leadership in charitable organizations, politics or public education.

- I want to retire when I'm 55 years old.

These have to be decisions based on what you feel will constitute living the right life for you. Then you should go for it! It will mean certain sacrifices on your part and the part of your family, but if it is the right thing to do, do it.

This makes me think of Shakespeare's *Hamlet*. How often have you said "To be or not to be"? "To do or not to do it"? That is the question. Here is the first part of the Soliloquy for you to enjoy!

> To be, or not to be: that is the question:
> Whether 'tis nobler in the mind to suffer
> The slings and arrows of outrageous fortune,
> Or to take arms against a sea of troubles,
> And by opposing end them? To die: to sleep;
> No more; and by a sleep to say we end
> The heart-ache and the thousand natural shocks
> That flesh is heir to, 'tis a consummation
> Devoutly to be wish'd. To die, to sleep;
> To sleep: perchance to dream: ay, there's the rub;
> For in that sleep of death what dreams may come
> When we have shuffled off this mortal coil,
> Must give us pause: there's the respect

> That makes calamity of so long life;
> For who would bear the whips and scorns of time,
> The oppressor's wrong, the proud man's contumely,
> The pangs of despised love, the law's delay,
> The insolence of office and the spurns
> That patient merit of the unworthy takes,
> When he himself might his quietus make
> With a bare bodkin?

Why quote from Shakespeare? Because I like this passage so much and to me it says you have decisions to make that are not easy, decisions that will probably not be understood by some and will be criticized by others, decisions that would be easier not to make and so not "suffer the slings and arrows of outrageous fortune." The decision to work toward becoming president of the company means a somewhat different life style. It means having fewer friends and it means many times not having anyone to talk to about things you need to talk about. You can make a lot of things out of what Hamlet is saying here, but why not make of it what is important to you? That should be "To be or not to be, that is the question." To live the right life or to not live the right life, that's the question.

Living the right life should mean living a successful life. Having these priorities and following these actions should create success in business and in life. But what is success? We asked this question earlier. What do you think it is? Here is what Ralph Waldo Emerson thinks about success:

Success

> To laugh often and love much; to win the respect of intelligent persons and the affection of children; to earn the approbation of honest citizens and endure

the betrayal of false friends; to appreciate beauty; to find the best in others; to give of one's self; to leave the world a bit better, whether by a healthy child, a garden patch or a redeemed social condition; to have played and laughed with enthusiasm and sung with exultation; to know even one life has breathed easier because you have lived... this is to have succeeded.

Isn't this wonderful? Go back and read it again and then share it with someone. Why not put this up on your refrigerator with the reminder about the priorities? Two magnetic crosses will look good in your kitchen.

Where do we find the definition of living the right life? The library is full of reference books and many friends have good advice. All are there for you to use and they're free. So is the Bible, and its messages are given to you freely. The difference is that the Bible comes complete with love, forgiveness and complete understanding. Let's use the Bible. Even if you are not a Bible reader, you can and should appreciate these messages because they are clear, easy to understand and undoubtedly right for both of us.

First, from the Old Testament come the Ten Commandments.

Remember that Moses, who was leading the people of Israel from Egypt to the Promised Land, spent 40 days with the Lord. During this time on Mt. Sinai, Moses was given the two tablets of stone, written with the finger of God. These contained the Ten Commandments. They are preserved in the Old Testament in two versions, one in Exodus 20, 1-17 and the other in Deuteronomy 5, 6-18. The following is from Exodus 20, 1-17.

I am the Lord your God, who brought you out of the land of Egypt, out of the house of slavery; you shall have no other gods before me.

You shall not make for yourself an idol, whether in the form of anything that is in heaven above, or that is on the earth beneath, or that is in the water under the earth. You shall not bow down to them or worship them; for I the Lord your God am a jealous God, punishing children for the iniquity of parents, to the third and the fourth generations of those who reject me, but showing steadfast love to the thousandth generation of those who love me and keep my commandments.

You shall not make wrongful use of the name of the Lord your God, for the Lord will not acquit anyone who misuses His name.

Remember the sabbath day, and keep it holy. Six days you shall labor and do all your work. But the seventh day is a sabbath to the Lord your God; you shall not do any work - you, your son or your daughter, your male or female slave, your livestock, or the alien resident in your towns. For in six days the Lord made heaven and earth, the sea, and all that is in them, but rested the seventh day; therefore the Lord blessed the sabbath day and consecrated it.

Honor your father and your mother, so that your days may be long in the land that the Lord your God is giving you.

You shall not murder.

You shall not commit adultery.

You shall not steal.

You shall not bear false witness against your neighbor.

You shall not covet your neighbor's house; you shall not covet your neighbor's wife, or male or female slave, or ox, or donkey, or anything that belongs to your neighbor.

What do the Ten Commandments mean today? These have to be as important to us today as they were to the people of Israel thousands of years ago. I think they mean much more because we have many more temptations today, have more opportunities to "steal" or, simply stated, to commit all kinds of sins. All the commandments have many meanings and degrees of seriousness. We need to realize that even with these ranges of seriousness, they still are commandments and should be followed. Living the right life means following the Ten Commandments.

During our trip to Israel, we had the good fortune to have an interesting and knowledgeable tour guide who spent the day with us going to Masada and the Dead Sea. It was a beautiful day with all of us on the bus thoroughly enjoying being together and listening to this enlightened woman tell us about her country and its history. As far as we were concerned, she could have taught and entertained us for the entire trip. She was a fascinating speaker with a fascinating subject.

One day we saw the archeological finds, including Masada and Qumran that are close to the Dead Sea. We visited Masada and as we looked out from its high desert fortress we could visualize the Roman soldiers around this mountain. They were waiting to conquer this seemingly impenetrable fortress and capture the 960 men, women and children who escaped from Jerusalem. These were the Zealots. We struggled with the question like so many other visitors and historians: Did these Jews flee to Masada in order to die on their own terms or to attempt to live, thereby continuing the lineage of the Jewish people? Being there one could feel their power, their insistence on integrity.

The Dead Sea Scrolls were found close by. Our tour guide showed us the caves where they were found. All of us had heard so much about the find, but I don't think we realized how many scrolls there were and how important this find really was. Parts of all of the Old Testament books except Esther were found in these caves. Our guide spent quite a bit of time explaining the significance of finding the Dead Sea Scrolls. She ended her lesson for us by saying that the Bible today is truly unbelievable because it is a translation of a translation of a translation of a translation of a translation and so on, yet it is exactly the same as was found in the Dead Sea Scrolls. The Scrolls were written in Hebrew, Aramaic and Greek. This information made a tremendous impression on all of us. This realization is a confirmation that the messages we have been given in our English Bible today are accurate. The truth then is still the truth today because the truth comes from the Truth.

I believe the answers for a successful life in business and personal life are a summation of the five priorities and the ten actions. Let's review them:

Give thanks that you have the opportunity, knowledge and motivation to live the right life all the time. Perhaps you need to do some fine-tuning, but you are basically there right now, and I hope this book will give you some additional thoughts concerning priorities and actions. Many people are not so fortunate.

Meanwhile these three remain: faith, hope and love; and the greatest of these is **love**. Living the right life has to be a life full of love and it has to show. You don't put love in a closet; you let it shine bright and clear. It not only has to show, it has to be shared with family, business associates, neighbors and, of course, God.

The LORD replied: "My son, my precious child, I love you and I would never leave you. During your times of trial and suffering, when you see only one set of footprints, it was then that I carried you." **Use the help** that is given to you freely from God. Use the help of your family and friends and your business associates. I think you can be successful in business only if you use all the help you can find from inside and outside your company or your organization.

For those to whom much is given, much is asked. We know this truth and it makes sense. God has given each of us our own special gifts and these need to be shared. Some have more gifts and some fewer, but all have gifts to be shared. Living the right life has to include sharing these gifts and **sharing in the right way.**

You have a **family** at home and you have a business family. You have your home life and you have your business life. Both are important in living the right life. What is most important is having the right balance. Your family has a much more important priority than your job, no matter what your job is. Even the job of the President of the United States is not as important as the president's family. No job could be. It is, however, important to be successful in whatever your job happens to be.

If a job is worth doing, it is worth doing well. Conscientiousness is also part of living the right life. The right life is family-centered first and includes success in the job. They go together; they are not in conflict. In fact they complement each other. That is what this book is all about: How to be more successful in business and in life.

God must be an integral part of living the right life all the time. Make Him a part of your everyday life, even at your job: "And, so I say to you: Ask and you will receive; seek and you will find, knock, and the door will be opened to you. For those who ask will receive, and those who seek will find, and the door will be opened to anyone who knocks." (Luke 11: 9 - 11) Jesus didn't say that maybe this would happen, He said these things will happen. Ask and you will receive, seek and you will find, knock and the door will be opened to you. God will be part of your life, if you ask. He will make sure you receive, find and have the door opened for living the right life.

When God has done these things for you, **don't boast, just let it happen**. This was the message in chapter eight, action number five. Remember the Golden Rule from Matthew 7: 12: "In everything, therefore, treat people the same way you want them to treat you, for this is the Law and the Prophets." Just be yourself, the self that you like and others like to be with.

There are many times when you question whether or not you should do something. Such questioning happens all the time in life and in business. Generally it has to do with sharing, caring or spending some of your time with or for others. The answer to this question is almost always yes, just do it. Do it joyfully and add **joy** to all those around you. There needs to be more joy in our world and you can make this happen. It is clear that great joy can come first from God and then from love, family and the satisfaction of living the right life all the time. "Praise God with shouts of joy, all people!" (Psalms 66:1)

Joyful people are also **grateful** and they express gratitude often. Maybe the two go together as they probably should. To me living the right life also means living a positive life full of joy to such an extent that it spills over on all those around you in business and in life. For that you can be most grateful.

Sharing grace with others is living the right life. It will benefit others greatly and will bring returns to you in many ways. It is like a special kind of chain reaction filled with good thoughts and actions that grow and grow. Little acts of kindness, **grace** freely given and received are ways to help us become more successful and live the right life. Remember in Matthew 5:42 Jesus says, "When someone asks you for something, give it to him; when someone wants to borrow something, lend it to him."

Earlier we discussed sharing grace by being truthful, trustful, dependable and considerate. We said these traits are very basic to having a well-performing organization that can be successful. Aren't these traits also necessary for a well-performing family? Aren't these traits also important for living the right life all the time? I think so.

Many of these priorities and actions can become so much more a part of our everyday lives if we make the temptations go away. We know what tempts us. We don't want temptations, we want to avoid them, and we want them to go away. It is okay to ask God to make them go away! All we have to do is say, "please God, just make them go away."

You can think of many of the temptations that bother you. They are different for each of us. In business there are also negative temptations and we call them objections. To be successful you want to make the objections go away. By being positive and optimistic and sometimes clever, you can make them go away. There are several examples I would like to share with you and maybe you will also share some with me.

An example occurred when we were trying to work out a partnership with Leviton Manufacturing Company in Long Island, New York. This partnership was to promote and sell a line of plugs and connectors for industrial applications. The largest competitor in the United States for this kind of product was Hubbell. They had a large market share but with a product that was not as good as ours. At least we felt that way. Hubbell's product had a few features that were different from ours and they also had a different material in the housing. We could demonstrate that our features were superior and our housing was of a newer, more modern material. The Leviton people kept saying that these were big objections and ones that customers would use to avoid specifying or buying our products. We felt that Leviton was using this objection to avoid entering into this partnership. Interestingly we had two objections working against us in this case. First was the objection of potential customers and the second was an objection from our future partner. Because of these two objections, we could see that this meeting was going nowhere. We called a time out and while we were alone discussed what we could do to make these objections go away. We had to make them go away.

We succeeded. We decided to make certain product changes so that we would offer all our good features and also provide the customer with the Hubbell features and at the same price. We also decided to use the Hubbell material for at least a few years during the product introduction period. Was this what we wanted to do? No, we really wanted to sell our standard product, but it wasn't going to happen. The objections had to go away. Sometimes to be successful the objections have to actually go away. They can go away if you are clever or you can be clever and wise enough to know that you have to make changes so that they actually do go away physically. There are objections every day in business. A good manager recognizes them quickly and leads others to take actions that make them go away. Don't live with objections that hinder progress and success.

You not only have to make the initial objections go away, you have to make the real objection go away. For a number of reasons, the objection you hear may not actually be the real objection. In this case you have to figure out what the real objection is and then have the wisdom and grace to make both the real objection and the voiced objection go away without terribly offending the person with the objections. Please give the possibility of unvoiced objections some serious consideration.

Let me give you an example of a time when we were up against an objection that wasn't the real objection and we corrected the situation and made the objections go away. A control engineer at one of the ABB companies in the Northeast selected and specified one of our competitor's products. When we found out, we of course tried to get the specification changed. The engineer defended his position by saying the competitor's contactors and relays were much easier to mount and thus the overall cost would be lower using their products. We disagreed with him, but were not successful in getting him to change his mind or his specification. His boss supported his position. We couldn't understand why he was taking this position until we discovered he had a friend who was with the competition and they worked together on this project. Our solution to this problem was really quite simple. We offered to provide our products already mounted in an assembly. We took in a prototype showing all the products mounted and it looked great. They couldn't use the objection of costing more to mount the products because there now was no mounting cost at all. The engineer and his supervisor had to agree that what we proposed was a significant cost savings to them and a way for ABB to use ABB products without the engineer losing face. We made the mounting cost objection go away. By working much more closely with this engineer in the future, our salesman and this engineer became friends. The other unspoken objection then also went away.

In life do what you can to make the temptations go away for you and your family. In business do what you can to make the objections go away.

Most of us have listened to many "children's sermons" where the minister is giving a short sermon for the children. Do you really think the sermon is for the kids? I know he or she is talking to me and is directing the message to children of all ages. It is effective. It is much like a list given to me by my friend Don Oden, who is retired in Grand Lake, Colorado, and driving a school bus. I want to share this list because it has so many good messages that relate to living the right life and caring about children. It isn't just for school bus drivers.

NOTES for School Bus Drivers to consider.....
   Provided by Don Oden, author unknown

- "Before I drove a school bus, I had about 50 theories on bringing up children. Now I have 50 children on board, and no theories."

- The greatest aid to adult education: children.

- Fifty years ago, parents were apt to have a lot of

kids. Nowadays, the kids are apt to have a lot of parents.

• Adolescence: When children stop asking where they came from, and begin resisting telling you where they are going.

• The mark of a good school bus driver is that he/she can have fun while being one.

• It is easier to build boys and girls, than mend them as adults

• Don't demand respect as a school bus driver. Demand civility, and insist on honesty. Respect is something we must earn - with kids as well as adults.

• It is better to bind children to us by respect and gentleness than by fear.

• Authority is a poor substitute for sound leadership.

• Rudeness is a weak person's imitation of strength.

• One of the best ways to give advice to children is to ask them what good things they want to do, and then advise them to do 'em!

• In the effort to give good and comforting answers to the young questioners, we very often arrive at good and comforting answers for ourselves.

• The only thing students who ride my bus find difficult to resist is - temptation!

• "Young man, are you trying to steal cookies?" "No sir, I'm trying not to steal them."

• Children are predictable. You never know what inconsistency they are going to catch you in next.

- Example is not the main thing in influencing young people - it is the only thing.
- Reasoning with a child is fine, if you can reach the child's reason without destroying your own.
- Children need models, not critics.
- To bring up a child in the way he/she should go, we need to travel that way ourselves once in awhile.
- The art of praising is - a fine art.
- Nothing improves a child's hearing more than praise!
- The sooner we begin to treat a boy as a young man... the sooner he will be one.
- Healthy, respectful relationship between adults and children are the best protection against the challenges of this modern world.
- A happy, healthy childhood is one of the best gifts adults have in their power to bestow.
- Respect the child. Be not too much his authority figure. Trespass not on his/her solitude.
- To punish and not restore, that is the greatest offense.
- The value of marriage is not that adults produce children, but that children produce adults.
- Students are often unreasonable, illogical and self-centered. Forgive them anyway.
- If you are kind, people may accuse you of being soft or having selfish, ulterior motives. Be kind anyway; gentle but never soft.

- If you are honest and frank, occasionally people may cheat you. Be honest and frank anyway.

- The good you do today, people will often forget tomorrow. Do good anyway.

- In the world of children - nothing is so severely felt as injustice

- Sticks and stones my break my bones, but names and words may break my heart.

- There are ways of listening to children which surpass compliments.

- Schools are places where teaching is not of the greatest importance - but where learning is of the greatest importance. The Superintendent agrees - as school bus drivers, and as a Department, we have a role to play in this mission.

* Watch your thoughts; they become words. Watch your words; they become your actions. Watch your actions; they become your habits. Watch your habits; they become your character. Watch your character; it becomes your destiny.

Living the right life all the time means keeping the right priorities:

- Love
- Family
- Joy
- Grace
- Forgiveness

Living the right life also means taking the right actions:

- Give thanks
- Use the help
- Share in the right way
- Give thanks to God
- Don't boast, just let it happen
- Be grateful
- Share the grace
- Keep the right priorities
- Live the right life all the time
- Follow me

Believing in these priorities and following these actions will ensure living the right life and becoming more successful in business and life.

Let's look now at the last action listed, "Follow me."

Take time to have wonderful and beautiful thoughts and dreams each day. Share them with someone close to you and who knows that together they might come true.

Chapter Sixteen – Action Number 10
Follow Me

The number 10 and last action is "Follow Me." "Last but not least" — I never have liked that expression. It is used way too often and usually the last is the least. In this particular case this expression is accurate. "Follow Me" is last and it definitely is not the least of the ten. It is number ten for a reason.

Who can say, "Follow me?" Well, anyone can say it, but who can say, "Follow me," and actually get people to do it? In the military if you were given an order to follow me, you would probably do it. But even in the military people have not always followed someone because they were ordered to do so! You would not always follow someone because he asked you to. No, you would want to ask questions and know more about where you were going. The truth is you follow someone because he is a leader and not because he told you to "follow me."

Jesus said, "Follow me," a number of times. Here are a few of these examples.

> And he saith unto them, "Follow me, and I will make you fishers of men". Matthew 4:19

> Then said Jesus unto his disciples, "If any (man) will come after me, let him deny himself, and take up his cross, and follow me." Matthew 16:24

Jesus said "Follow me" to a number of people; some did follow him and others had reasons why they just couldn't accept his invitation at the time.

> And he said unto another, "Follow me. But he said, "Lord, suffer me first to go and bury my father. Luke." 9:59

> But Jesus said unto him, "Follow me; and let the dead bury their dead." Matthew 8:22

> Jesus said unto him, "If thou wilt be perfect, go (and) sell that thou hast, and give to the poor, and thou shalt have treasure in heaven: and come follow me." Matthew 19:21

Today if Jesus said to you, "Follow me," what would you do? I think you would have to question what does "follow me" mean in a practical sense? Where will we go and for how long? What should I tell my family? Who will provide for them? Do I have to sell all that I have and give it to the poor? I think what Jesus would mean by saying "follow me" is that He wants to be your leader, a very important leader of course, but not one who is going to ask you to leave your family or your job or to sell all that you have. He wants to lead you in the right way to be successful in business and your personal life. He wants you to follow these ten actions and five priorities. He wants you to know that He is the way.

What is a leader? A leader is, of course, one who leads. And, by definition, one is leading only if there are followers! Let's look at some thoughts on leadership.

In our new office and training center we have some motivational pictures and messages on the wall. I think they are effective if people take the time to read the messages and think about what they have to say. One of them has to do with leadership:

The Essence of Leadership

> A true leader has the confidence to stand alone, the courage to make tough decisions, and the compassion to listen to the needs of others. He does not set out to be a leader, but becomes one by the quality of his actions and the integrity of his intent. In the end, leaders are much like eagles...They don't flock, you find them one at a time.

Do you have some messages about leadership that you would like to share with me? Please send them to me along with your other ideas.

There are leaders and there are followers and sometimes leaders are followers and followers are leaders. It depends on the positions and circumstances. For instance, you might be a leader in Church and a follower in your job. Or it might be you are a leader in little league baseball and a follower in the United Way campaign. In business it is very likely that you are a leader and a follower at different times.

Here, we are talking about being a leader, not a manager. A good manager is also a leader, but just having the title of manager does not make the individual a leader. A manager can ask employees to work for him and follow his instructions, but he cannot ask his subordinates to follow him. "The Essence of Leadership" says the manager does not set out to be a leader, but becomes one by the quality of his actions and the integrity of his intent. You earn the right to be a leader. You earn this position of leadership by doing the right things. The right things are all included in *Time Out...It's Your Call* given to you in this book. You know about them.

Think about the leaders you have known and what made them good leaders. I think I first thought about leadership in high school. The ones who were "leaders" in high school probably were the most popular persons because they got elected to be cheerleaders or president of the student council or some other such position. Actually they probably were not the real leaders because they did not attain their positions because of their leadership abilities. An example of a real leader in our high school in Des Moines, Iowa, was Randy Duncan, who was the quarterback on our football team. During the fourth game of the season in our senior year right in the middle of a huddle, Randy said to all of us, "This is what it's all about! We are going to win all our games this year." He was clearly our football team leader. We all knew it and you know we also all knew we were going to go undefeated and be the Iowa state champions. With his leadership we were the best we could be. We ended the year as we expected - 8 wins, 0 losses and 0 ties — and were voted the number one team in the state. I think all the players on the team felt this was the high point of their life at the time. I know I did. I also know that everyone on the team knew who the team leader was and there was no jealousy about Randy's position of leadership. Randy went on to become an All-American quarterback at the University of Iowa and led his team to win the Rose Bowl.

This is an example of having the right leader at the right time with all the team members happily accepting his role of leadership. That is the way it should be for leaders.

In the "Joy" chapter, I told you about my good friend Jim Truba. Jim decided to retire this year, and during his last week at work he sent me a letter. I would like to share with you what he said:

> Dear John:
>
> Tomorrow is the last day of my formal working career and I couldn't enter my new retirement life without expressing my gratitude to you for making my past life so rewarding. Under your leadership (better stated partnership) I experienced my most productive times. The greatest compliment that I could give you I have already tendered by copying your management style. I would describe it briefly as hire good people, give them direction, recourse them, fight off that which may tie their hands and get out of the way. OK you might like to follow their activities up on Fridays with a few wines but that's just showing that you care. I appreciated the opportunity that I have had working with you and look upon it as the apex of my career.
>
> Best Wishes,
>
> Jim

I really appreciated receiving this note from Jim. I liked what he had to say about hiring good people and then making it possible for them to succeed. Isn't that what a good manager and leader should do?

What are the traits of a good leader? Develop your own form to list what you think are the most important traits or characteristics of a good leader. The form should have columns for you to rate yourself and to mark areas where you feel you need improvement. A few of them might be found in the following list.

A Good Leader

- Leads by example - walks the walk and talks the talk
- Is a good and compassionate listener
- Usually is a spiritual person
- Probably is a reader
- Thinks of others first
- Is a good communicator - considers always who needs to know and who thinks they need to know
- Communicates at the right level of difficulty to ensure understanding
- Knows where he or she is going and wants the team to share in the vision
- Is a winner and develops a winning team
- Is honest and can be trusted always - expects the same from the team
- Is not afraid to ask questions - it's okay to say I don't know
- Is one that team members are proud to introduce as "my leader"

- Has a sense of humor - doesn't take himself or herself too seriously
- Is intelligent enough - willing to have more intelligent people on the team
- Is a quality person - attracts quality team members
- Is knowledgeable about the business
- Takes great joy in the success of the team members
- Makes opportunities available to employees - is a giver in the company
- Is an optimist
- Probably has a very happy home life - is successful in life as well as in business
- Enjoys knowing about you and your family
- Is an opportunity seeker - not risk avoider
- Has empathy and can put himself/herself in the other person's shoes. Can feel their pain.
- Is a "good" guy or gal - know what this means? This is important.
- Enjoys life and it shows

This is quite a list! How many more items have you added to your list? How do you rate yourself as effective in all of these traits? Remember, this list is about being a good leader, not a good manager. In today's business environment I believe you have good managers who are not good leaders. Please think about this statement for a minute.

Now please take a blank sheet of paper and write the names of those who you feel are good leaders. This list of good leaders should include people you have had association with from the past or the present. How many do you have on your list? Do you have any? My guess is you have very few. You know why? I think it is because we don't have many really good leaders in our business world today. You might not have any or very few in your company. There just aren't enough to go around. It's like good quarterbacks in the NFL. There just aren't enough good ones to go around. You see more good leaders in your personal life than your business life. Don't you agree?

Shouldn't good managers also be good leaders? It would be great if this were the case. You surely would want your manager to be a good leader. What can we do about the lack of good leaders in business? This is one of the main reasons why the book *Time Out...It's Your Call* was conceived. If managers would follow these ten actions and keep these five priorities, they would be on the way to becoming good leaders. You can help your managers to become good leaders by sharing this book and letting these managers know you believe in these priorities and actions.

At the beginning of this chapter I mentioned that "follow me" was the last action but definitely not the least. When I first became aware of priorities and actions, there were five priorities and only nine actions. I questioned if there shouldn't be ten actions. The answer I received was, yes, there should be ten and the tenth action is "follow me." I also questioned if "follow me" shouldn't be the number-one action. The answer was, yes, it should be first, but if you were given "follow me" as number one, you wouldn't get to the other five priorities and nine actions. You would either be scared or wouldn't believe what was being given to you. God knows all about us and obviously knows what He is doing.

Life is so precious for everyone. Doesn't it make sense to have priorities in our lives? If we agree priorities are important, then isn't it also necessary that we have the right priorities and take the right actions to be successful?

Chapter Seventeen

Using Priorities and Actions

We have discussed the five priorities and the ten actions with examples from personal life and business life. I'm sure you had many similar experiences that probably came to mind as you were reading this book. I hope you took the time to make note of them and will send them to me so they can be shared with others.

There were many suggestions given to help you follow these five priorities and take these ten actions. The intent was to present them in such a way that they could naturally become a regular part of your personal and business life. It was also the intent of this book to have written lists so that you could monitor progress on a regular basis. Now it is up to you to decide what you do with Priorities and Actions in your life.

How many training sessions, business meetings or motivational programs have you attended where there were some good ideas presented? You have good intentions of changing some behavior when you get back to the office, but somehow it just doesn't happen. Good intentions get pushed aside because more urgent matters need your attention, especially after you have been away at the training session. There are many monkeys running around that have been looking for you. Before you know it another year has gone by and you find yourself in another course with the same good intentions again. Maybe you actually never get around to using the course material in the form it was presented in these programs, but you still gain something. You have new and fresh ideas that are absorbed and become a part of your subconscious to be used at some appropriate time in the future.

How about *Time Out...It's Your Call*? Do you think the five priorities and the ten actions will be valuable to you? Will they help you to be more successful in business and in your personal life? Can you accept them as they are? Do you think you need to modify them in some way that would be better for you? Is the concept right for you to have a list of actions and a list of priorities that you should follow? Will using these lists help you to become more successful in business and in your personal life?

Do you now have a definition of success? Do you know what it means to intensify your success in business and in life? Each person should develop individual goals and objectives to achieve success or become more successful. Priorities and Actions should be part of this process.

You know the sayings: "No pain no gain;" "You get out of it what you put into it;" "Nothing ventured, nothing gained." Following the suggestions given in the book will require some effort on your part, but if you become more successful in business and your personal life, won't the effort be worth it? If you have started using the lists, great! I hope you will continue and do even more as you see the results come in. If not and if you were waiting until the end of the book, why not start right now with just one list and give it a try?

Some closing suggestions:

- Thank someone today - someone in business and someone else outside of business.
- How long since you told someone close to you that you love him or her? Do it today.
- Are you struggling with something or some problem right now? Can you involve someone and use his or her help?
- Is there someone at work or in your family who is struggling with a problem or an assignment? Can you share with them?
- What joyful thing can you do today?
- How can you share your grace today?
- Who needs to hear "I'm sorry" from you?
- Does your schedule for this week need to be rearranged based on your new priorities?
- Please send your experiences and contributions.

I hope you have found *Time Out...It's Your Call* to be of value to you and your family. God bless you!

Time Out...
It's Your Call

Order copies of this book for those that you care about: family, friends, neighbors, business associates, church members, schoolmates present or past, members of your favorite organizations and community leaders.

You can place an order by mail, fax, web or phone. Please send your order to:

    Bridgman Consulting   Phone 940-692-4007
    3610 Glenwood   Fax   940-692-4007
    Wichita Falls, Texas 76308 Web   www.bridgmantimeout.com

Please send me _____ copies of John Bridgman's book *Time Out...It's Your Call*. The price is shown below plus shipping and postage of 3.50 for the first book and $1.00 for each additional book shipped to the same address. Texas residents please add the sales tax as shown.

        Number of copies _____

        Price each   _____

        Sales tax (Texas) _____

        Shipping cost   _____

        TOTAL   _____

Price Schedule:

    1 to 4 copies $24.95 each
    Tax (Texas)   2.06 each
    Shipping   3.50 + $1.00 for each extra

    5 to 24 copies $22.45 each
    Tax (Texas)   1.85 each
    Shipping   3.50 + $1.00 for each extra

    25 to 99 copies $19.95 each
    Tax (Texas)   1.65 each
    Shipping   3.50 + $1.00 for each extra

    Over 100 copies   Contact Bridgman Consulting for prices

Shipping Information:

    Ms./Mrs./Mr. _____

    Address   _____

    City/State _____ Zip_____

    Phone #   _____

    Email   _____

Payment is enclosed or please charge my:

    Visa   _____

    MasterCard _____

    Expiration date _____

Thank you for your order!